Grief and The Light Within ~
Year One

By Lisbeth Chapin

John —

Knowing that the light of our mothers still shines upon us.

Peace to you here)

Betsy

April 2016

If you are grieving ~ You have my deepest condolences. Your process deserves honesty and respect, from yourself as well as from others. This is a journal I kept for five months during the year following the death of my mother, at 88, for whom I was a primary caregiver. If you can think about beginning a daily writing practice of your own, you may find it a helpful way to unburden your own thoughts each day; I did not expect mine to do that, but it did. Every journey of grief is as distinct as every person, and I know that losing a mother is different from losing a child, a partner, a sibling, a father, a friend, even a pet, or more than one of these together. Whatever your circumstances of grief, more than anything, I hope that this journal helps you navigate through the days and months ahead. These are uncommon hours, and you are somewhere, alive, within them. The entries that follow do not minimize the loss; rather, they explore it deeply, day by day, inside an ordinary life – a job, a dinner, my backyard, a grocery store. May the words in this journal honor you, the one you lost, and the love you had together; that love, too, is intact somewhere and honors us all.

If you seek to comfort a grieving person ~ I recommend that you first be present with and listen to that person; just being with someone who is grieving is a gift to both of you. Sometimes companionable silence alone is a balm. It is often a comfort to talk about the loved one, but not everyone wants to do that right away; be willing to follow wherever the conversation leads. Grieving people need their own privacy, time alone to reflect, to feel what they need to feel, sometimes for many months. Keep in touch regularly with that person; if there are disrupted eating or sleeping patterns that concern you as a friend, talk about your concerns with the grieving person. Respect the journey of grief, the profound experience of it, and wait for your grieving friend or relative to tell you what she needs. "How can I help?" is one of the most important questions anyone can ask, and be sure to follow through when that question is answered. You don't need to have all the answers for anyone's questions or to have what you think are the right words to say; very little of that matters. Just be willing to occupy with the grieving one the space she is in, even in silence; you are helping her heal. Love recognizes love, and he will never forget your gift of it.

If you seek information on grief counseling or support groups ~ At some point, you may wish to consider pastoral counseling, traditional therapy, regular visits with your faith leader, grief support groups, or a combination of these. For more information beyond referrals from family or friends, explore professional directories, such as the American Association of Pastoral Counselors or the American Psychological Association. As well, reputable hospice facilities and funeral homes often have grief support systems, including recommended counselors. Grief is a complex experience, and a professionally trained counselor can offer a perspective that helps stabilize you enough to remain functional, week to week. If you feel isolated in your grief or that it is straining your relationships with others, consider talking to a professional counselor, whose guidance can help you regain your emotional balance. [See the end of this book for a list of websites.]

Acknowledgements

I am not sure that this book would exist had it not been for the support and direction of its first audience, Donna Strachan-Ledbetter of the Brandywine Pastoral Institute. Donna's encouragement to gather my journal entries into a book, a book that potentially could help others who grieve, was empowering and affirming and changed not only the life of my grief but also my life as a writer. I am deeply grateful.

I also owe a sincere debt of gratitude to Diana de Armas Wilson, who cast a keen writer's eye on each phrase, each sentence, and each entry; because of her careful attention, this book is better than it would have been. In addition, her own experience of grief made her an invaluable reader and added immeasurably to my perspective on the subject. I write here also to thank Carolyn James; her generosity in reading this manuscript through her own deep grief not only enriched our friendship but also this book. I am grateful, too, for the comments provided by Patricia Hoge in her recent widowhood and those by Christine Eberle, as well as the support of the clergy and members of Trinity Episcopal Parish of Wilmington, Delaware.

I am very thankful for the kind and attentive listening ear given these entries by my family members, close friends, and several students; their patience and thoughtful respect for my efforts was more appreciated than they will ever know, reminding me that, to some degree, a true writer writes to *all* readers, wherever or however a book finds them.

Most of all, I am eternally grateful to my beloved parents, Patricia Maher Chapin and Robert Stuart Chapin; from them, I learned that life is worth cherishing and celebrating, even though it can be unpredictable, unfair, and difficult, even devastating, yet that some form of recovery from loss is attainable and that all healing begins and ends with love. In truth, they taught me that love is a big, ungainly book with many chapters, and, in their lives, they read to me from it, every day. They inspired this book, and I hope, wherever they are, they know that I am reading those chapters back to them, page after page, day after day, in the home of my mind.

This book is dedicated to ~

Lisa Kay Martin
(1979-1996)

Patricia Maher Chapin
(1923-2012)

Robert Stuart Chapin
(1918-2003)

René Carr Pauley
(1950-2014)

Introduction

"As if..."
        "As if..."
            "As if..."

In transcribing my journal of days, I was struck by this phrase that I wrote so many times, trying to describe my thoughts and feelings of grief. As with good poetry, to write about grief is to put into words what cannot truly be put into words, so we reach for metaphors, similes, anecdotes, images, incidents. We get near it, but words are as hummingbirds to the blossom – moving toward it, humming into it, but not exactly bringing forth the flower. That's where the reader comes in, a reader who understands beyond where the words can go. As it is, our arms are full of bouquets, those of us who are grieving, and we are waiting for the words to come into them, retrieve what is vital, and carry that indefinable substance back out into the world.

Soon after...

Soon after my mother died, I was sitting at my computer, staring out the window, as the breeze rippled the water in my bird bath, when I felt something very close to me. I felt time itself pass by, as if it were a person, and in its wake, I was within a stillness so serene, so rich, so silent, so impermeable, I knew that I was at some boundary of the physical world. The breeze ceased, the water no longer movable. It was so still I seemed to hear God breathing – where time and God met -- and in between breaths, no time.

This was the border of the world without my mother. And I had to cross over it.

In the aftermath of the first weeks, summer settled into me, and the warmth lulled me into its own rhythm of days: attending to my flowers, reading the newspaper, meeting a friend or family member for a meal, working in my yard, brushing my cat, preparing dinner, watching television; I have very little memory of any of it. One day, my ankle twisted in a crevice next to my deck, and I fell, scraping my arm down a concrete block. The 15-inch abrasion bled down to my leg, and my arm later swelled up so much that the green, blue, purple, and yellow bruising was quite a sight. I remember looking at it, surprised that part of me was still alive in the world.

My swollen and discolored arm was no less strange to me than my being here.

Early in July, I had an urge to be in the water, to swim every day (I rarely swim). I joined the YMCA and a class of low-level water aerobics -- all women, all middle-aged, just like me. The instructor would give us direction, and we would bob and move around with our

Styrofoam floaters, only our heads above the water, chatting. We heard all about our instructor's trip to Alaska, and those of us farther from her in the pool would strike up a conversation of our own. About two weeks into the class, I mentioned – to the damp face of one of the women near me -- that I was in this class to help me get through the grief of losing my mother. She nodded soberly. I relaxed my head back against the water, hearing the cloud of conversation above the pool, and, at that moment, the afternoon sunlight angled in from the window and entered the water. It held me there, and I knew then that I would find my way back, back to feeling alive again in my own life, even starting at this surreal distance, among these strangers, in this unworldly space.

Before it all...

I lived with my mother and father, then in their 80s, when I moved back home to Delaware from Denver, after graduate school, at age 44. In the ensuing year, as I taught English at a private high school by day, I would work on my dissertation in the evening and on weekends, and I continued this into the summer. My father would be at his desk in the bedroom opposite my own, scrutinizing his stock reports, and I would be writing arduously until dinnertime. We two worked companionably that summer of 2002, every hot and humid day, balanced each to our own side of the second floor of the house. I have not known the same kind of working peace on any project since.

My father, a research chemist, and I were sympatico, as they say, both intellectuals. He found the world endlessly fascinating and inspired his six children also to find it so. This former lieutenant-commander of a Destroyer Escort in World War II understood the danger of taking risks of all sorts, and this chemical engineer embraced the value of education with the zeal of one whose parents had not had that opportunity. He was very supportive of my research, my degree even though begun at age forty, and my efforts to complete my dissertation. I was grateful beyond words. He and I each maintained a strict regimen during our daylight working hours, and no three people were happier to join each other in dinner at the end of the day than he, my mother, and I that summer.

Sometime into the winter, shoveling snow and ice, my father broke his arm; not long after, he was diagnosed with cancer, primarily in his colon and his bones, later into his brain. I cared for him with my mother. We did the best we could, but he suffered stoically, then suffered beyond that, then finally lost consciousness and died; it took five months.

This book is not about that time, not that grief. That experience was not one I could write about, nor may ever write about, because what

I saw was too painful to review and describe in length. Someone later said to me, "It must have been difficult watching him die," and I remember staring back, speechless. *Watching?* There is nothing passive about being present for and nursing a person who is dying. I did a great deal more than watch: I lifted him, steadied him, encouraged him, asked questions, prepared food, supported him in walking, drove him to appointments, reminded him, called doctors (sometimes in the middle of the night), dispensed medications, monitored developing conditions, questioned nurses, spoke to doctors, applied and timed each of the dozens of morphine patches, helped with personal hygiene, facilitated visitors, spoke to family near and far, updated family with emails, ordered medical equipment, and managed bills and accounts, among other duties. The grief was thoroughly physical, mental, and emotional; it began months before my father left this world and continued for many years afterward, sometimes expressed as a kind of rage, more often as depression. Three years later I sought counseling for it, but I wish I had done that sooner. The trauma of the caregiving experience combined organically with the grief of losing him, and it took time and guidance to disentangle them and then rework them into something I could live with. That kind of trauma and grief blasts like a series of explosions into the bedrock of you, and you are forever fundamentally changed, which, I suppose, is as it should be.

Our family laid my father to rest, and my mother and I began our life together, remaining in their home of thirty-six years. For the following nine years my siblings and I cared for her, and while she had several serious conditions, she was always ambulatory and able to continue a fairly active life into her eighties; eventually, some of her medical issues prompted cognitive and emotional decline. When she became less steady on her feet and fell one day in the house she loved, I realized it was unsafe for her to continue to live there, even with me. She moved into a senior community, Forwood Manor, for the last six years of her life; I lived near her and continued much of her care.

In these smooth sentences, I do not mean to dismiss the difficult and consuming job of being a caregiver for an elderly parent, whatever the complications. It is more than consuming: rather, your life is subsumed into it, and you are daily changed by it – not the core of you but certainly the first ten layers of who you are, on any given day. And I did not do it alone, by any means; one of my sisters lived nearby and was very much involved, and my other siblings contributed regularly, as well. In any case, there were many, many mornings, afternoons, and evenings when caring for my mother was overwhelming, was mentally and emotionally exhausting; when being on call and placating her anxieties and solving her medical problems that day was almost beyond what I could handle, mentally or otherwise; after nine years of cumulative effect, I was nearly done in. I was heard to say that it must be taking years off my life, and I meant it; the stress worries into every crack and crevice of your psyche and is unlike any other kind of stress. It is a kind of relentless pressure, a refined, unending tension that inundates the mind, that pools secretly behind thoughts, and lingers threateningly under every emotion; it is a climate change of the psyche, which, nevertheless, must surge imperfectly forward and orchestrate the loved one's care.

Yet there were many happy afternoons and evenings, much emotional intimacy, regular and constant visits, weekly lunches and dinners at our favorite restaurant; and our relationship became closer and deeper each year. We understood each other, we inhabited each other's daily life, and we enjoyed each other's company.

Grief does not need a perfect relationship; it works with what is left and sifts through every fiber of that fabric, where color once was, where design once held. There were many days in caring for my mother when I could have been more patient, less irritable, more responsive, less complaining, more forgiving, more willing, and less impatient, it is true. I have absorbed that knowledge of myself and moved forward with it. I also have learned that every caregiver has the same kind of regrets, and that they are unavoidable. Those who have never performed a caregiver's role cannot comprehend the entirety of the experience and only judge, sometimes ungenerously, from their limited perspective. Those who have performed that role share a kind of camaraderie, deep in our bones, and we all understand each other.

In May of 2012, my mother suddenly took ill with what we thought was a stomach flu, later diagnosed as pancreatitis. Following the successful removal of her gall bladder, she suffered complications and passed away, two weeks after entering the hospital.

The Summer 2012 Olympics ...

In the first few weeks and months of grief, a person may feel as if moving through some unexplored depths of an ocean, floating in a murky world, muted around and above. I was submerged in grief, and I had no idea how I had found myself there. Eventually, after many weeks and tides and hours, I began rising through it, discerning a surface and daylight. Even so, I rested in the lull, observing the world above me.

In late July, the Summer 2012 Olympics burst into the world and through my television, startling back to life some part of me. All the water and light of the world seemed to be thrashing around in those pools; I was entranced. I began looking forward to watching each event every evening and intently followed all the competitions. I remember this very clearly as the first happy thought that I had experienced since my mother died; its very entrance into my consciousness was unexpected and brightened that small road that our mind travels down every day to get to evening. I was still in the water exercise class at the Y, and we members chatted about the Olympic events, my swollen arm feeling the achingly cool water, our dripping suits rising from the pool, satisfied with our own feats.

If I could have lived continuously in the ocean of my mind, the water at the Y, and the pools of the Olympics, never emerging entirely from any one of them, I would have. But life goes on as if your grief never occurred, and you must pull yourself up into the air of life, at some awkward moment, in order to feel natural on firm ground again.

This journal...

I began this journal seven months after my mother died and four months after I had begun teaching at a new school, a job whose transition from my earlier one was a daily challenge. I worked sixty-plus hours a week teaching, planning, prepping, grading, writing up forms, helping students, going to meetings, adjusting to the systems of the new school -- not unlike many teachers in this country do each week; inevitably, it would have been difficult to move from being a professor with some measure of autonomy to being a teacher at a private high school, but achieving this during a grief recovery was nearly impossible. I loved my students, but something within me was collapsing. Thankfully, I sought counseling, and my therapist suggested I write about my experience every day. At first, I dismissed this, but I decided to give it a try: What did I have to lose? Now I would recommend it to anyone who is grieving. Once I started, I began to long for the hour each evening just before sleep, when I would open my journal and, in complete freedom, write into the center of my own mind. These entries are what followed, as truthfully and honestly as I could write them, as clearly as I could record the experience.

They were written not only for myself but also for you, to offer respect for the grieving process you are moving through, to give others insight into the condition of grief and its complexities, and to acknowledge the extraordinary world that we inhabit, within and without. May these writings give you a clear light within which to rest and find peace, until you emerge into the freedom of your own days.

January 6, 2013
Sunday

The odd thing about grief is that you realize
how much *space* there is in the world – mental
space, emotional space, physical space even. I
notice how much space there is in the sky with
one airplane flying through it, like a single
thought moving through God's mind. I see how
much space is between each branch on a
winter tree – the dark and delicate branches
through which I see the crystal blue and white
sky. A hawk flies over my house as if in years.

The unfrozen pool of water in my bird bath: the
birds and I know it is the most perfect,
coherent thing among us delicate, space-
intricate, feathered creatures; we are smaller
than thought, and more alone.

January 7, 2013
Monday

TRUST GOD. That's what the sticker read inside the car window, as I watched it go through the car wash in front of me. I found it comforting. I have felt an awareness of the spiritual realm since I was a child, so "God," to me, harkens of that realm, heard within silence, a silence that falls into a sentence like sunlight through a window – subtle, true. My task is to listen, access, discern, feel, move forward. For this, I go back to myself as a child, an afternoon of sunlight in a room, birds under a picnic table, clouds over a swing set, the moon sleeping in the sky.

I have to exit time itself, then wait.

January 8, 2013
Tuesday

My day was dead. Each hour rose dull and murky, as if resisting the clock. I was tired, fatigued so emotionally and mentally, it was as if I had forgotten the language I was within, a foreigner in my own day.

I thought of my mother this evening, as I prepared a dinner for me and a guest – baked fish, biscuits, green beans. How many dinners did she prepare? How many saucepans did she look into? How many faces eating robustly? How many days and hours did I share with my mother and my family that are within me, somewhere?

January 9, 2013
Wednesday

"You were very good with her."

Meg, the theology teacher, said this to me after overhearing a conversation I had with a senior about her college application essay. It was gratifying to hear.

I am somewhere inside the day, but so rarely do I feel it that I am distinctly taken aback when others see it.

Off I go – into another night of the dream realm – my greatest freedom.

January 10, 2013
Thursday

I was remembering that every Friday night my mother would ask me if I needed anything at the Dollar Store. Once in a while I would think of an item or two, but I didn't usually need anything. My mother was happy when I could think of something, so I often tried – or she got me some items anyway, when my brother took her there, most Saturdays. My mother loved me in many ways – deep, ordinary ways.

In the afternoons, in her apartment, I would clip her fingernails and toenails, since she could not manage this herself anymore – we would laugh at something in the act of doing this.

Sometimes it seems that the deeper into winter we go, the further I get from myself.
To what end?
(To what end?)

January 11, 2013
Friday

I attended the funeral of my friend's father today.

A neighbor of the deceased, originally from Coventry, England, told me that she was weeping while we sang the hymns because both hymns were ones they would sing to fortify themselves while the Germans were bombing near their home; she recalled her mother's face, crying. All those voices, still singing, all that love within her, still glowing – it filled my face.

There are moving energies under and around all of what we see in life – in conversations with mourners, in a baby's glance, in an oak leaf blowing across the street. There are presents and pasts throughout every moment, energies of love and doubt, grief, kindness, and the sadness of the past, settled within a man's broad shoulders.

January 12, 2013
Saturday

Today, I wandered through Barnes and Noble, searching for gifts; I found what I needed — three books and a sign language kit for my friend's nephews. It was gratifying to see their pleasure opening them. By being in it, these boys make me feel better about the world.

Isn't it affirming to feel that the most important flow of energy in the day is exactly what you think it is — love? It invigorates any moment in any ordinary day and leaves behind a circle of peace in the heart, an ease. It is always the simplest -- and most perfect — choice. I was different afterwards.

January 13, 2013
Sunday

In church, listening to the organist –
Sometimes an ordinary moment drops into the
eternal, dips down like a sound wave. The air
shifts inside a musical note, and the moment
floats within, somewhere in the room.

It's a recognition of one note to its parent
realm, the eternal.

In the state of grief, you are silhouetted against
the doorway to eternity. If you are very still, it
becomes part of you.

January 14, 2013
Monday

I remember sitting with you in the office of
your eye doctor, outside the exam room,
watching the television. Sitting and waiting in
all your doctors' offices never bothered me,
you know. I read, usually, while you watched
the people around us.

Aquariums, tables with magazines, couches,
deep chairs, strangers assembled, arbitrarily —
life at low tide. It seems to instruct us, waiting
for the nothingness we are lulled into, so
something can begin.

How alone, how vibrant my love for you, sitting
in our silence.

January 15, 2013
Tuesday

A huge emptiness when I settled at home this evening – it nearly strangled me, emotionally. How to become water and pour through one evening? I sat and meditated for about fifteen minutes, but the nothingness stilled all dimensions – no messages, no images, no thoughts.

("Nothing will come of nothing." *King Lear* 1.1)

I hear the rain falling, a comfort on this long, dark night.

I am emotionally diminished – resigned, accustomed, feeling time like homework.

January 16, 2013
Wednesday

I am attempting to meditate every afternoon, to calm my emotions and try to connect with the realm that I was so naturally a part of, as a child. How do I alter myself back to that state? I am calm; I am trying.

Tonight when I called and left a message for my brother, I was about to ask, "Are you taking Mom to the Dollar Store on Saturday?" For several seconds, I actually believed all was as it was. The memory was so pleasant, so soothing, I rested there for a while. I wish I could rest within the child that I was, my own (more serene) mind.

Off to the dream night, my other sanctuary.

January 17, 2013
Thursday

Grief really is a form of afterlife, because those who are grieving can never again regain the life they had before. One is reconstituted by grief into a different life, and never a better one.

There are no "gifts" to be had from losing a loved one – it is neither a privilege, nor a blessing – inspiring no coy smile about the wisdom or enlightenment visited upon you.

It is loss, silence, air, loneliness, stillness, evening, afternoon, dinner, emptiness, full darkness – an opening to all distance, all time – and you must move forward, by the inch.

January 18, 2013
Friday

There is exactly half a moon tonight.
Remember when we would look out the bay
window in the dining room every night, before
we went to bed? All your life, you loved gazing
at the moon, wherever night found you.

You said that the worst thing about your
apartment was that you couldn't ever see the
moon.

I gaze at it tonight, in a vibrant night sky. I'll
never forget the two of us standing by the
window, silently accepting the lovely moon and
its shadowy glow, accepting all the quiet love
between us.

January 19, 2013
Saturday

You would have been with us tonight, at our birthday dinner. You would have gotten spaghetti, after asking me what you usually ordered. You would have made us all laugh at something funny. You would have had some of the yellow cake with chocolate frosting and a cup of decaf tea, no milk or sugar. You would have gotten me and Laurie each a birthday card, with "Lots of love, Mom" written inside and a check that I would have written for you. I would have looked into your brown eyes and seen that you were happy to be there, in the center of us.

I wore your ring tonight, and the diamond sparkled on my finger, the diamond Dad picked out in 1945 at the PX on the Navy Base in San Diego, two weeks after you met.

I only feel at home in the world in the cold night sky, with the moon shining to me like a face in a room.

January 20, 2013
Sunday

It is 12:01 a.m., so our birthday has just ended. When I consider our birthday, I believe all three of us were born together, in a way. You were born to us, as we emerged from the womb, and Laurie and I were born together, with you. The three of us were never the same; we all heaved into a new realm from where we had been. If that is called birth, have I been birthed into grief?

The reason people sometimes want to change their lives after suffering the loss of someone deeply loved is because their life feels so foreign, and they seem to be a stranger within it. They make drastic changes not to move forward but to lurch back – a shift with such momentum, they are hoping it heaves them back in time.

But neither the present, nor the past, nor the strange new world they now inhabit can be occupied, because they have been birthed into "the undiscover'd country" (*Hamlet*) – in this case, not life after death, but the afterlife of grief.

January 21, 2013
Monday

Today was President Obama's second inauguration, attendant with all the pomp and pageantry one would expect. But I was in a place with equally as elaborate procedures and pacing: I visited my friend, René, in the hospital, where he is recovering from a bone marrow transplant. That is difficult enough, but submerged under that is his grief for his mother, for whom he was caregiver and best friend, the last twelve years. She died last month, while he was having chemotherapy, and he could not see her for some weeks before that because of his compromised immune system.

I went to her funeral – I will never forget René sobbing behind his white mask; he was devastated, especially at not being able to say goodbye to her. Her funeral was our farewell to her.

That farewell to our loved ones is why we, the grief-stricken, desire only to be left alone to stare out of windows and glass doors for hours: We are watching them go.

January 22, 2013
Tuesday

It is quarter to midnight on the coldest night in two years, they say. I have never longed for warm months as I have these past weeks.

Something in me believes that when the seasons shift and things around me start growing, the activity will enfold me within it, and I will be less obvious, will appear less dead, will feel camouflaged by spring. If everything is moving and growing around me, what difference – what matter – if I stand so still in the air, as if under ice?

The leafing of trees near me – it is company; the birds, conversation.

January 23, 2013
Wednesday

Another cold night, and I worry about the cats in our church graveyard, those that people have abandoned and we feed. What or who else is cold tonight, abandoned, alone, feeling the chilling nothingness of the night air on their face?

Who are we, who live there?

It is as if the cold finds *us*, knowing we have created a space for it, detectable even in the afternoon sun.

January 24, 2013
Thursday

I miss giving you my arm, when we walked.
Do you miss my arm?

You steadied me, too. When we walked like
that, all else fell away, and pieces locked
together.

I miss sitting at the lunch counter with you. I
miss walking into your apartment's lobby and
seeing you sitting there, chatting with friends. I
miss stopping by after church for our special
visit and doing your meds for the week; I miss
driving with you next to me, watching the
clouds.

Once again, it's a frigidly cold night in a dark,
clear sky. The moon glows round and nearly
full. There is nothing but the sky, the cold, the
moon, the quiet – a quiet as if a personality, a
sentinel against the day of life, a quiet of the
soul of night, solemn in knowing that we, all of
us, return to it, majestical and stark.

January 25, 2013
Friday

The moon is full tonight, but we cannot see it for the snow that fell lightly this afternoon. It is a cloudy night, again very cold, but a natural winter night. The moon rests, hidden in the darkness.

What natural element am I in, when I move in the winter night of grief? Where am I?

In teaching *Twelfth Night*, I told my students that grief can be an identity, a pain that becomes its own costume. Am I on the outside of it or the in? One is re-costumed in grief, and it seems to me that some part of me recognizes it and moves incrementally within it, as the moon moves somewhere in the cold night.

January 26, 2013
Saturday

I went about my duties of caring for you – in
your apartment, in the health care facility, in
the hospital room – like a nun in a sanctuary. If
I had been lighting candles, filling basins of holy
water, or laying out the altar cloths, I could not
have performed my tasks more efficiently or
more reverently. This is not because I was in
awe of the presence of serious illness, or of
being in a hospital or a facility; rather, it settled
on me like a calling, an impersonal calm, a
sustained focus to do what was required.

Not all forms of love become a purpose, but
mine did for you, as if I had memorized my part
and rehearsed it, from the first minute I was
required to step into it. I ministered with
tender respect, unfazed by commanding
nurses, distracted doctors, dazed visitors, the
avalanche of instructions, the awkward white
of blankets and beds, by procedures, staff
changes, and policies; amid all, I did not waver,
resolved by the love in which I stood.

January 27, 2013
Sunday

My grief and depression pressed down upon me so heavily today that my chest hurt to breathe, and I was sick to my stomach, or nearly so.

When I saw the character of a young woman in the television series *Downton Abbey* die this evening, I remembered identifying your body laid out in the funeral parlor before they cremated you. Every day in the hospital I had traced a cross lightly on your forehead with my right thumb. When I did that to your forehead in the funeral home, your skin was so cold it burned the tip of my finger; I recoiled, then felt guilty about that, so I returned to you in that large, silent room before we left, to rectify that feeling. I decided to ask if the funeral home assistant could cut a few locks of your hair for us, which he did. I have them in a small, purple, velvet pouch in my jewelry box.

The cold burn on the tip of my thumb lasted for hours, until I fell asleep that night.

January 28, 2013
Monday

The most significant moment of my day was when I offered my arm to an elderly nun, an Ursuline sister, who was visiting us today. She was about to navigate some steps, precariously, so she took my arm and my hand – and smiled up into my face. I could not speak, and my eyes teared; I was as helpless, in my way, as she. My nine years of purpose in helping you are not gone, only in suspension.

I know what it is to come home to an empty house.

I know what it is to stand alone in a room looking out at trees, a sky, some cardinals, as if they were waiting to land on me, as if I am as plain as a dark branch, waving very slightly in the opaque afternoon.

January 29, 2013
Tuesday

I exist only in looking out, frozen in grief. My therapist today encouraged me to write my thoughts and feelings in my journal especially in these conditions; I agreed. What else is there to do?

I know what hopelessness is, how it comes up over you, how your own house can seem dead, as if the furniture in it were not yours, had never been yours; all the vibrancy of your life darts out a window, and you are left in the shell of a home, as dusk falls.

January 30, 2013
Wednesday

The ordinary of the everyday – it's something to hold onto, to reach from one hour to the next.

Take the trash out on Thursday. Fill the bird feeders on Saturday and Wednesday. Put out the recycling on Monday morning. Feed the cats before breakfast. Clean the bird bath, empty the litter box, turn on the dishwasher, stop at the grocery store, stop at the hardware store (for what?), stop at the drugstore. I do these things because they need to be done, small burdens that make me weary. But they gain their own momentum, and I hope that somehow the movement of these tasks will dissipate my grief-sodden afternoons and mornings.

A necessary task should take precedence over a state of mind, shouldn't it?

Wasn't that the case for all the years of my caregiving, when the necessary tasks that were required of me superseded my reluctance to do them, my desire to be simply a visitor, instead of a worker?

What is it now that I take care of? At the center of these ordinary tasks is no ailing, infirm parent.

If I am unwillingly doing these simple, necessary tasks, when all I want to do is sit in a chair and stop time, what is in the center of my sacrifice? What is requiring me to keep moving?

I resist the tiny drop of satisfaction I feel from completing any mundane duty. I resent the ordinary day's pretending to be ordinary – *how dare it?*

Grief instructs me: There will never be another ordinary day. But the duties required of everyday life keep me attentive to the new patient – the Nothing that I tend, in my own time.

January 31, 2013
Thursday

The air in my home felt friendlier tonight, and I moved through the evening more easily than of late.

I entered into the usual corridor of emptiness when I walked through the door, but my cat, Patrick, came streaming forward, and I realized how much I missed him. We formerly spent long afternoons together, before my schedule changed, and I was happy to greet him, as well as my other cat, Lucy, when she appeared on the stairs. The air shifted.

After I exercised, I sat on the floor to meditate. My usual scene is to imagine myself sitting against a tree and staring into a creek in front of me. In doing this, to my surprise, my mother walked up to me, smiling. Her face was fresh with happiness and love for me; then my father was there, too, also smiling. I absorbed their message: they love me, they want me to know they are aware of my troubles, and that they can be with me, just as when the three of us lived together so happily – that I am, in a certain and real way, not alone. They are in my realm and send me love. I felt their presences, their personalities, so strongly that I was deeply comforted.

I have now and again in the last nine years intuited my father's presence and several times in the last seven months my mother's presence: all of a sudden, someone is there, just checking in, then gone. But this was a deliberate visit, and they wanted me to know we are still "a good team," as Mom and I used to say of the three of us. And we were.

February 1, 2013
Friday

The month that I claimed as "My January" is over, and I am grateful to have gotten through it. At the end of December, I could not face how I could endure a long, cold, bleak month ahead. All I envisioned were empty afternoons and the frigidly cold air closing me in like cell walls, reminding me that I was trapped in this schedule, this job, this season, this loneliness of grief, these aggravations of teaching, these roads, my route to work, the same parking spot every day – even the kitchen clock itself – all seemed to conspire into a message: You are a machine, and we are programming you, the automaton, where and how you go, what you do, how you do it, when you do it, how often, how well, and you must simply operate by these instructions, these prescribed paths.

That is what a normal life feels like to a grieving person, who is on such a different track that it is as if that person is on a monorail above the city. How do grieving citizens, who look normal to others, conduct themselves within a normal life?

We are not on the same route as you, even if you see us driving on the highway. We are not eating the same food, walking down the same street, feeling the same sunlight on our faces. No matter how fluidly I go about my life, in speaking, teaching, driving, washing a bowl – I am not the same person; I am not in the same universe. I move through yours with you, but I am not there. The machine you are trying to program into a normal life is a camouflage comprised of the first ten layers of grief, those levels of shadow that, astoundingly, you see not at all.

Only the cats come through the shadow to approach me; I love them for it.

February 2, 2013
Saturday

I learned today that, some years ago, a friend
and colleague of mine almost died in a near car
accident. She remembers thinking, in some
lucid moment, that she was going to die. But
someone – an angel, she believes – guided her,
unharmed, through the intersection.

That surreal calm, that precipice, is familiar to
the grieving person. We have peered into it,
have felt the cool eternity of it. We know that
this is where evening comes from, and
midnight, and dusk. Our souls recognize home,
tenderly, and we wonder what else in life we
have not yet seen, entirely.

February 3, 2013
Sunday

One friend told me that someone she knew had a dream in which her recently deceased uncle visited her, saying, "your aunt is not doing well; she needs help with this [his death]." My friend said the niece told her aunt, and that her aunt was somewhat dismissive and not much comforted. My friend wondered why that was so. I tried to explain.

The belief in the hereafter, even in such a specific incident, is among other things, intellectual, while grief is of the heart. Knowing my own mother is happy again, in spirit, with my father, makes me grateful, but it does not make the grieving state less intense, once it settles in. Time must take part in things here; grief is *caused* by time, since it separates us from our loved one –
we, too, are a "one"
a loved one
isolated at still being alive.

February 4, 2013
Monday

As I was talking with a colleague today, I could feel myself detaching from the conversation; it was so mundane, so boring, I could barely continue to speak. What, I wondered, keeps people connected to their day? How can such a conversation exist? It was as if the world went silent, and I was watching two women talking.

The layer of energy behind a conversation, a thought, an idea, an expression of the face – that is where I live and search, lost, here where the topsoil of life is so foreign, and I wait all day to vacate it so I can arrive into the evening, among all of history, and rest in its limitless depths.

February 5, 2013
Tuesday

I used to come home and see my phone light
blinking to show I had a message (or several)
from my mother. Now I come home and all is
solid – no blinking light, no messages. I gaze out
at a backyard as still as stone, a sky as solid as
the ground. It is as if nothing is waiting for me
or notices I am there; it is as if I was never
there, in any time.

I am walking through a house that I do not exist
in. I stare at other silent things.

Gradually, I feel the quiet acceptance of trees.

February 6, 2013
Wednesday

When I am rising from full sleep into consciousness, I am in something like the lobby of the mind – where two states of mind meet. It is quite serene, yet active mentally; I am most comfortable in this state, where no one asks anything of me, where my mind can move by its own tides.

Grief creates its own lobby, not unlike this state of mind; it is where the mind, emotions, and spirit meet. Grief slows your mind to an ancient tempo, an old peace. It is the peace of loss – the stiff emptiness that has its own dignity, a state where silence is like a weather system, and stasis an exultation, the purest rest.

February 7, 2013
Thursday

"All things exist as they are perceived: at least in relation to the percipient." P.B. Shelley

I wondered today what reality is. Is it when I hear a train whistle far off in the winter night, and I am strangely comforted because it seems to echo something from my childhood? Is my mood the reality, no matter what my surroundings?

How is one to determine what is real from what is imagined? Even the emotions demand interpretation. The scent of impending snow in the morning air − and I remember a snowy day in second grade, Mom, when you walked to school to bring us our boots to walk home in. I was struck by that gesture, even as a child. I wish I could speak to you on that day – to see what you saw out the window, to feel your impulse to venture out into the heavily falling snow that afternoon, to know what you thought about on the mile walk to our school. I can still see your face, holding up my white rubber boots, smiling, in the school hallway. I realize now: You were happy to see me. You knew that day what you loved and what you wanted to do.

The faintest scent of snow this morning was the most sharply real moment of my day.

February 8, 2013
Friday

Grief is in the body. It is a raw pain at the center of the rib cage, in the solar plexus. One must, every day, grieve through this permanent abrasion in the heart, must breathe through it, hundreds of times a day.

In breathing through it, you have the vague conviction that you are moving, as if you are walking through a town at night.

Surely, you feel, I must have made some distance; surely I must have covered some ground, must be on the outskirts of town by now.

But here you are in your own home, on another evening just like the last. With every breath, you settle in for the night.

Your grief is your home now.

February 9, 2013
Saturday

There is a bag of your clothes in my bedroom
closet, the bag I brought home from the
hospital. I cannot bring myself to empty it,
although it has been eight months since I
brought it home.

I'm sorry I didn't rush over faster, when they
called and said you'd fallen, that you refused to
go into the ambulance, but that you were very
weak. Something in me resisted, unlike the
other times when I drove to you, in a panic, the
momentum of both of our lives still in effect.
This time, although I arrived within the hour, I
found you changed, when you looked at me, as
if some part of you had already left the room.
Two weeks later, at 1:31 a.m., June 13th, on the
sixth floor of the hospital, you lifted away from
this life and into the night of the mind.

Your apartment has been emptied, your things
dispersed, but I lift and hold this bag and the
clothes I helped you out of, and what I was,
inside my life with you.

February 10, 2013
Sunday

Grief is organic, shifting with the hour of the day, with the light in the room, with the company one keeps. It has its own expansion and retraction and is unique to each person who experiences it, although we all understand each other. The stages are definable or not, and not in any declarable order, necessarily. If stages, then I find they are repeated, and, if different, they are subtle.

Oddly, it also seems a continuous surprise. I know, because of my experiences of the mystical , that my dear mother and father are together on the other side of life, in spirit and love with God. My disbelief is here, on *this* side. It is easier for me to believe *that* spiritual reality than the reality that they are not here.

Grief instructs me, daily.

February 11, 2013
Monday

A year ago, tomorrow evening, I took you to church for the Shrove Tuesday pancake supper, remember? We enjoyed the pancakes, and you had sausage, too, and decaf coffee. It was the last evening function you went to, at Trinity. I enjoyed being there with you.

Tomorrow is Shrove Tuesday, and the dinner is planned at church. I am anxious about going. Am I supposed to pretend that it doesn't matter that we were there together last year? Am I supposed to simply get on with life, placated by "our time together" and be thankful, then just move on, complacent on every other Tuesday hereafter?

So much a part of what makes grief real is an acknowledgement from others of the loss suffered, of others being familiar with the person who was formerly with us, that others know we were never this alone before. Grief radiates out from us in discernible ways, energies that seem to push back, no matter how ordinary the day or how humble the plate before us.

February 12, 2013
Tuesday

Shrove Tuesday supper tonight was pleasant, though it was empty of you. Now that you are no longer here, it just felt as empty as everywhere else – my living room, a restaurant we always went to, my car. Everywhere feels like the same element – did it, before, when you were here, I wonder?

Sometimes I cannot disentangle my other emotions from my grief. My ennui, weariness, anxiety, impatience, frustration, worry – they do not rise from the grief, but grief fills in the area all around these woods, and when the leaves are in the air and the wind picks up, it's all the same ecosystem.

Everywhere is one place, in grief, and that one place is consciousness.

February 13, 2013
Wednesday

To the grief-stricken, the word *no* is always easier, always at-the-ready. It comes from a general dejection toward life. Grief is the most profound form of discouragement. Will things work out for _____ (anything)? No. Will I have the money to _____? No. After all, the most significant thing in your life – your loved one remaining with you – did not work out, so why should the more mundane things in life do so?

The natural inclination is just to stop. No answers, no remedies, no solutions rise to the surface. And the general activity of life seems merely like water over ice – nothing is really melting.

People will say, "well, death is part of life," but they are entirely wrong. Death is its own realm – and, in a way, none of our business – but it is certainly not in life's energy; it is the total absence of life, and it should seem strange, foreign, and indefinable to us. And no matter how many times I witness and recognize death, it never seems natural, not a part of anything except itself.

The tedium of grief is in its favor, actually. That tedium of the mundane and the continuous is most like life itself. The grieving person has stopped in the flow of life, but knows it is streaming around her. At such times, the only desire is to be like other living things whose organic existence stays in one spot – a boulder, a tree, an evergreen bush that the birds rest within.

February 14, 2013
Thursday

You'd think being on this earth for over fifty-six years, I would have something continuous from my past around me on a holiday such as this. But as my mother and father are gone, and since I saw no one from my family today, it might as well have been the first such St. Valentine's Day of this life.

But grief reminds me otherwise.

I remember coming together for dinner on an ordinary weeknight of February 14th, a holiday that my mother thought should be special, no matter what day of the week it landed on. She bought each of us a little gift and made a cake with pink frosting for dessert. This warm celebration was a true balm in young adulthood when neither my sister nor I had a boyfriend. Mom turned it into a happy evening, just being in one another's company, in our home.

Grief is the most intimate connection to our past. The territory from that to our present is more than in years, but in that territory we know that the deepest truths dwell, silent and calm.

February 15, 2013
Friday

Grief begins itself. It moves to its own dictates
and schedules. Its entrance into consciousness
is a mystery. It may begin somewhere in time
before the loved one's death – a week before,
months before, an hour before. Grief comes in
when it is needed, respectful, comprehensive,
efficient – in total command before you are
even aware that it has entered the room. It
knows you intimately, and you begin to feel
that it has been in the room your entire life.

Grief can come at the instant of death, the
shock that carries you over a boundary of your
life before and your life after, because you
could never have arrived there on your own.
You remain in disbelief for some time (cherish
it).

Grief can begin so subtly, incrementally, as if in
thin seeds, after the loved one's death, that
you finger those seeds in your mind to
determine the cause, but its very pervasiveness
begins to take authority. And then you move
within its realm, and there is nothing in your
body or yourself that rejects it.

February 16, 2013
Saturday

Are you ever happy? Someone asked me, after
our conversation about grief. I said yes,
thinking of a recent dinner with my sisters,
during which my focus was on them and our
love for each other. It was on a winter's night,
when the darkness seems to have layers. Our
love together held that place around the table,
and the warmth of it seemed to radiate out into
the evening atmosphere, repelling all forms of
darkness.

The ways of grief are with one person at a time,
are complete in one person, perpetually. They
can recede, for a while, but their territory is
vast and unfathomable.

One person becomes a universe.

February 17, 2013
Sunday

I don't want to meet anyone new – because
that person never met my mother, and I am too
uncharitable in imagining how she would have
liked the new person or not. I only want to go
where she went, drive where we drove, walk
down the same corridor of a restaurant.

I have no energy to imagine her in a new place
– nor to imagine myself in one. I do not belong
here, in this present, unless grief centers me
back to the knowledge of where I once was.
There is no other existence except that, with
my body or my mind.

February 18, 2013
Monday

An unexpected feeling from grief, for me, is a consuming sense of personal inadequacy. Whatever grief is, you are unprepared for it. You are not adequate to the occasion, not up to the task, not capable of handling the full extent of it, so we simply must give up to it. Since both of these states – feeling inadequate and giving up – are slippery stones to stand on, neither is accomplished, at least to any discernible degree. Neither is natural to ordinary life.

It is not your fault, and you are not irresponsible to find yourself in this state. The grief is yours, personally, as if it were designed for you, and is as bewildering.

Grief continuously feels as if you have forgotten something, as if you are trying to catch up to something, as if you have left something unattended.

This kind of personal anxiety is as if you heard the crash of a huge building months ago, and are just now remembering it; this jarring of time's dimensions is inexplicable. The death of a loved one is an earthquake, and it is many months before you even begin to realize what buildings have fallen.

February 19, 2013
Tuesday

By the afternoon, the day thins – into a narrow trail of where to go, what to eat, what room to walk into. A conversation feels as if each word is a building, and you are trapped in an alley.

Finally, alone.

Dinner is over, and I know I am alive because the cup of tea is warm in my hands. I gaze into my cat's fur.

Grief is work, and it is best completed alone, when one can submerge into it, making you feel that you must study it – as a philosophy that turns in on itself: you follow where it leads you. Grief requires deep attention, at the beginning of day and at the end, in the stilted afternoons, and through the dreaming night, its natural state.

A grieving mind resists consciousness, but in the morning knows that the day will gather its own momentum and flow like an eddy into a crevice, into the cave where the soul waits.

February 20, 2013
Wednesday

Although in grieving I don't know the way,
every street is the same; space has its own,
new dimension, and time has its own laws.
Every grief is organic, although it feels the
furthest thing from nature; you begin to envy
the incremental nudge of the bulbs against the
soil far below. There is nothing as decisive as
the stem of a crocus, you realize. All nature
moves in one direction, and it seems to move
through you to wherever it is going – to the
appointed day in its season.

You are so still, even the sunlight doesn't
recognize you.

February 21, 2013
Thursday

Grief creates a space between you and the life
around you – and inside that space is a cool
dusk, an eternal afternoon, air without
movement or sound.

Someone is driving home in grief this evening;
someone is preparing dinner in grief; someone
reads before sleep in grief, hoping that in
drifting into unconsciousness, the grief, too,
will sleep.

Many woke up in grief this morning, will drive
down a road in grief, will lift things and choose
things and conduct their daily tasks and
business as they need to.

And all the while, grief sends out replacement
energies of itself, to maintain the infrastructure
between you and everything moving around
you, because, in doing so, it holds at bay the
searing pain that stops your lungs from
recognizing oxygen, that revolts against every
other part of your body that cooperates with
the universe.

February 22, 2013
Friday

It is a Friday in February, cold and damp, but without any snow, wind, or other weather drama. It simply continues cold, as if a Friday in February will continue forever, resisting the ordinary, cyclical day. Does grief belong in the element of cold? Does it have seasons, as nature does? Is it natural, or does it exist alongside nature? Is a grieving person more *in* the world or out of it?

Loving someone gives us hope in the world, equally if someone loves us. Although the person may no longer be here, alive, the love for that person continues. This love burrows through the darkness to the other side of the living world, and in this mystical territory, it does not waver. In fact, love strengthens and defines the new darkness, reassigning it now as a living continuum. The grieving person is filled with a love that travels a great distance and expresses itself here as a great echo, a calling, seeing, feeling, hearing of a loved one – another dimension of different senses; grief attests to the furthest reality: love as something to live into, connecting this life to the next – exactly what it knows how to do.

If grief is love with seasons, we cannot fathom the length of its days.

February 23, 2013
Saturday

My sister and I talked last night about missing our mother. We understand the depth of that feeling in each other; we understand who she was. Is grief collaborative, then?

Words move lightly on the surface of grief, so whatever my sister and I say to one another, it is the life behind each word that conveys more of the experience. Grief communicates by permeation from the inside, radiating outward to the boundary at the edge of one's skin. While grief crosses this boundary to intuit the world around it, it is not always recognized by others; it deserves to be so.

The way you used to hold your chin in your hand, watching the mourning doves feed at your window, while contemplating the clouds – none of that truly can be encompassed in words, so how could the absence of you, formerly three feet from my chair, possibly be articulated?

Grief is indeed collaborative: It is heard with every mourning dove, seen in every cloud, felt in the vacant light of every window.

February 24, 2013
Sunday

Grief is expansive in the psyche, so expansive that it has already become the only atmosphere in every room. When I walk into the kitchen, I forget why the air feels as if it is missing a dimension. It seems a long way back to remember when the air felt full again, with enough emotional oxygen.

Misery makes us contract, and grief inclines us to wish to fold in on ourselves – a folding in, over and again, until we come to the center of something, inside a darkness as comforting as the womb. Here, we could hope to rest, out of time, out of anywhere, unmissed, unnoticed, breathing inside the depths of the universe.

February 25, 2013
Monday

Sometimes grief peaks in a public place, and there is nowhere to go alone to express it. Today mine surged in a sudden feeling of anxiety and nausea.

Grief is a condition; its waters rise and fall, and sometimes the terrain drops off, so that you are swimming up to your neck, until your feet touch ground again. There doesn't need to be an obvious trigger; there are great mysteries within it.

Grief is a condition, not a mental illness, although a faint twinge of embarrassment seems to rise off of those around it, if not within it. On the contrary, a grieving person offers society a chance to meet the human psyche face to face, in its most complex ecosystem – profound grief – immeasurable, unknowable, except for the exotic birds occasionally glimpsed flashing through the trees.

February 26, 2013
Tuesday

Each day in grief is different, as unique as any other day, even though we sometimes feel grief to be a region through which we move as somnambulant figures. Yesterday, I was knotted up with a roiling of emotions; today was more placid. I mentally sifted through the detritus, as much out of habit as out of a need to order and analyze. And what sense can I make of it, after all? Can I wander through this ornate experience with any sense of direction or control? Can I tell someone else going through it that it will end soon – or end, at all?

Your body, self, and soul move into grief, eyes closed, as into an ocean, and shift slightly, imperceptibly, with the smallest current.

February 27, 2013
Wednesday

From a distance, grief may seem to be a vague, shadowed realm, a solid sort of dusk, if dusk could have substance. But a grieving state can actually feel like an erosion – some part of you, a part on which your day balances and rests, erodes on a daily basis. Oddly, it also erodes your sense of reality, your understanding of time; you no longer accept its limits, since your mind settles in the past, with your loved one, while the medium of grief conducts you into the present, unhappily, unavoidably.

You can feel the eroding, the burning – as you read, as you walk, as you speak, as you pray. Sometimes this vortex of change interrupts the desire to eat or sleep – which is understandable. But the body reminds you that you are still alive, that whatever erodes the emotional substance of you is at odds with your still-beating heart, expanding lungs, moving hands. Neither of these conflicting states is satisfied. We breathing creatures, of assembled parts, accept the grief-- corrosive or calming -- whose shadows of energy connect us with the living, every unwilling hour of every day.

February 28, 2013
Thursday

I wish I wore nothing but black for a year, as they did in earlier times, as a reminder to all that grief continues for many months and years. I wish people could see what a grieving person looks and acts like – because they then could perhaps reconcile the two – an ordinary person behaving normally most of the time – yes, we generally behave and act as normally as everyone else.

Most people might imagine a grieving person as one at a funeral, but what about that same person six or eight months later? Where do you see the grief? Or do you not see it? We will not usually grieve in public, so our grief is submerged and undetected. How would wearing black in my dress or with an armband shift the relationship with those around me? We need to bring grief back into the ordinary day: the grocery store, the school board meeting, the restaurant.

Grief pours out of me every day in a thousand minute radiations – so the black for mourning would only confirm and manifest that which you may already intuit and respond to, something that may yet sleep within every observer. I want the black clothing to invite you to look not just at me but at your own deep potential to hold loss daily, familiarly, next to your skin.

March 1, 2013
Friday

I'm astounded that time has pronounced the arrival of this month and puzzled that part of me is alive enough to see it. What is spring in nature? A thousand movements – squirrels, daffodils, trees, cardinals and robins – their lives burgeon, over and over, every day.

But how is spring experienced inside a person? Do our bodies and minds correlate with it? March is an intelligence of activity, and I marvel at every small and certain stem rising from the earth.

Grief listens – not just to a woodpecker on a tree or a calling blue jay or a subtle breeze. Grief listens even to the dawn, to the sparrows and their light, in another backyard, in another year, my father and I together one March morning, watching every bird and branch, as time moved over us. We listened, and I hear it now: Grief loves the company of spring.

March 2, 2013
Saturday

A grieving person is a balm to the world.

Grief observes and intuits, listens and divines in others what might have gone unnoticed before. The subtleties of human interactions rise into a new dimension, and their intricate movements and messages come forward – we witness glimpses of feelings, details, stories half-expressed or remembered, those you expect no one to be able to see. We notice what is unspoken or half-begun, a memory flitting through the heart, the pieces of a life delicately gathered and carried into the day so that the afternoon is a path we can walk down and not a wall to climb over. There is something in you that we turn toward instead of away from, a recognition, a love of someone moving over your face, and we offer a still moment for its grace.

March 3, 2013
Sunday

I wonder if there is anything more intimate than a voice? A voice is contained and conducted in the air around us – physically vibrating our eardrums, traveling directly down "the natural gates and allies" (*Hamlet*) to the heart, the mind – it meets our face. Physical absence, at least for a time, we are accustomed to, but the voice is not something we ever expect to be separated from, nor can ever prepare for.

How I would love to have a conversation with you, to hear your voice, even over the phone, talking of what you had for dinner or some memory we enjoyed together.

I want you to know that there is no substitute for your voice in my life, nothing that can resonate anywhere near the same way in the uniquely empty air of my heart.

March 4, 2013
Monday

People will say, "as long as you remember your
mother, she lives, in your memory." I'm never
quite sure of the full extent of that statement.
If I lost all my memory, does she cease to exist
here, in this dimension? Well, she does not live
in this dimension, to begin with; I have felt her
spirit's presence several times – just dropping
in to check on me (I feel her in a cheerful,
loving mood) – but she exists in the afterlife,
with God, in my belief.

Even so, if all memory of her were drained from
me, what would remain within me of her love?
How am I forever changed by my mother's (and
father's) love, whether or not they ever "live"
in my mind?

Whatever substance our love for each other
created in the loved one, it remembers this and
"harkens after it" (J. Donne) when a memory is
revived. I can feel more loved and secure in the
world when I imagine them here with me or
when I remember a happy evening together. At
such times, their world is also my world, and I
am peaceful.

My mother's and father's love resides in me,
activated into some element received by my
soul and applied to establish me as a more
coherent being here on Earth. Some part of me
circles around it, with a faint hope that their

love exists most as a presence within me,
expanding to meet me.

March 5, 2013
Tuesday

There are twelve calendars in my home, eleven on the wall and one desk calendar; I find them comforting, in some way.

Grief seems to create a feeling of floating between your past and your future. The past is a place to go to every day in your mind; in fact, it's nearly impossible *not* to go there.

The future is unknowable but in a completely uninteresting way; there is nothing alluring about it, at all.

Strangely, the present is as unknowable as the future. This expansive vacancy I float within only grounds me occasionally – the mailbox, a glass of wine, my cat.

It is as if I am en route somewhere, cast off, with no memory of leaving the station. Will I arrive somewhere, like spring?

March 6, 2013
Wednesday

Although grief is caused by the passing of someone deeply loved, it is also strangely impersonal.

Most of the time, I am not thinking specifically of my mother, but I exist in a parallel universe that resembles my life except that it is without her. At the same time, it is like driving through a strange neighborhood for which I have no feeling at all. This atmosphere – and I do not mean physical surroundings – feels less intimate than a hotel lobby, at times. The loss of my mother precipitated it, and I walk within this impersonal realm, one that seems to silence every natural thought and impulse.

It is almost as if I must behave impersonally within it. This could be why others detect a detachment, of sorts, in the deeply grieving.

Of course, the distant thought is that if we are quiet, courteous, uninterested, and uncaring enough, Grief will find us tedious subjects and move on to someone else's life.

I wonder – how would we notice, if a shift occurred?

March 7, 2013
Thursday

It is March 7th, which means that my niece died
seventeen years ago on this day; she was,
herself, seventeen.

At the time, it was inconceivable that she could
be gone, and the reason, the failure of an
internal organ due to an illness, did nothing to
make it more believable; it is still inconceivable.

There is moving space between the event of
death and the loved one. The state of her being
gone is something solid, but the death itself –
no matter the degree of violence or peace –
remains always inconceivable and unknowable.
I believe that as the soul departs the body,
there is a falling back, as if in water, as all one's
worldly worries and concerns fall away; it is as
fluid as any place can be – and in its own part of
the universe. But as to the finality of their
death on this side of the realm -- none of it is
anything that we can entirely accept, no matter
in what year or in what particular conditions it
occurred.

Maybe that's why grief is so confounding: it
retains a permanent mystery, an impenetrable
darkness, those waters that now determine the
true continuance of grief – familiar and
inevitable. To accept grief and live within it is to
concede that it is profound and pure and resists

all understanding, imperiously. We, ourselves,
must simply lie back within it and float.

March 8, 2013
Friday

To be in grief is to feel as if you have a job;
there are tasks that you must take care of every
day, almost mechanically. And you wait.

There is a strange feeling of "doing this until" –
until what? If you faithfully do your daily tasks,
you believe something will accumulate in your
favor, and the inevitable result would be that
you would get your life back.

To grieve is to hold onto your past so strongly
that you almost believe you can pull it into the
present. Work of all kinds can assist. Diligence
is a friend to grief, a kindness in the form of
repeated activity. No one can take away from
you the work you choose to do. Death takes a
loved one away and is completely out of your
control. In response, we fill our hands and
minds with work, and we wait. We are so
mechanical that a part of us could be sleeping
in order to carry out the tasks required. In
truth, the sleeping part can only tolerate being
in the present if the past is the loving world
determining all our choices.

I wonder if our grief gets bored with us? By the
time we realize what we have not had the time
or inclination to do that day, everyone has left
the room.

March 9, 2013
Saturday

People may look at those of us grieving, see our vacant expression, and think we are stuck in time.

The truth is that time seems to slide off of us.

There are days and days that become weeks through no natural system, a version of time that is secret to those who have never grieved. Each minute is like a day, and when the afternoon finally arrives, we have no memory of when the day began.

Conversely, a week can pass as if it never occurred.

Time is not fluid for us as it once was, but we grieving ones prevail. We prevail because to be alive is to do so, to line up at some border of evening, so that when some invisible arch of an hour sweeps over us, we will be there, accepting, if we can, the merging into the ordinary order of days.

March 10, 2013
Sunday

The tinge of sadness that I heard in a song
today is as if from far away; it harkens back to
its source, the most profound of all loss, what
all intuit but experience at different times and
at different levels. We grieving know its source
and are only beginning to be immersed in the
full ocean of its depths; we see currents there,
feel distances no land could accommodate.

We sing below the song.

March 11, 2013
Monday

Sometimes I'm not sure whether grief is positive or negative. To others who grieve as I've experienced it, there is a deep response and empathy to each other and our words about it.

To those who have not experienced grief this way, there is little response, except to consider it as an idea, and perhaps even an uninteresting one.

People generally have sympathy when I share my words written here. I appreciate that, but sympathy is my least favorite response; I'm also somewhat surprised by it, since I am not writing for that purpose. I write more to put my hand into the weave of life and finger the threads and fibers and get to know my own multi-hued system; in this, I sense that others have similar threads and textures, and I write to affirm this.

Grief is a subtly intense experience, and perhaps I seek to engage on these deep levels in order to feel that I am not alone in these dark corridors – where all the positive and negative energies of life conduct themselves and flow through us.

March 12, 2013
Tuesday

It is the end of a long day – of rising with duties ahead of me; in and around a day of teaching, conversations, grading and preparing classes, reading, exercising, preparing a dinner with my guest, making cookies, more reading, and several hours' worth of work left undone. I woke up tired, and I will go to bed tired. I will wake up tired tomorrow morning.

It occurred to me that to live in the world with a mother no longer alive is to begin a second life, since the first life began and ended with her beating heart, breathing lungs, moving thoughts. Every day some new aspect of me feels as if it is coming into form and other aspects are being refined. The sense of her near me is a shadow around them all. My resting thoughts tell me this.

March 13, 2013
Wednesday

An ordinary day requires a lot of energy, it seems to me – to do the work required for your job, the work at home – house, pets, and yards – and all the navigation and interactions with others, outside the home. Those who are young or not grieving have what seems an unbounded energy on which their lives run. They have a buoyancy of hope, love, and security. Once grief or other emotional hardships are experienced, that energy is not automatic; it has to be ordered, re-established, installed, and implemented.

I feel some days that my energies are very depleted, and the sense of my mother as a presence within which I could feel secure in the world has fallen away. It's almost as if we grieving are echo-locators of emotions; if the sonar doesn't bounce off anything or anyone we know, then we detach, and the connecting process slowly gets settled again, since solitude has its own energy.

Is the degree to which we grieving ones use energy different than others, or do we just have more places for the energy to hide?

March 14, 2013
Thursday

We are halfway through March, and it is getting harder to concentrate, although I don't feel inclined to analyze why.

Sometimes I worry that I will tire of the ordinary in life, and the ordinary is where we live most of our lives. It is also where the best memories are hidden and rise into the mind, which is soothing to a grieving person. The ordinary days and routines are things upon which we lean every day, and I usually find them comforting. Being in a state of grief, at whatever stage, is to expect nothing to be able fully to comfort you; everything falls short, and you fall into a kind of resignation about the effectiveness of words or gestures that could break through it. I suppose even the ordinary in life becomes less than itself – but it is the first place I am looking to, to seek the depth and fullness of love that left with my mother.

To grieve is constantly to seek an ordinary life – or an "ordinary" that we can live with.

March 15, 2013
Friday

I felt anger today over a friend's ignoring my feelings in a situation, when the other person made the kind of blithe decision that can impact a relationship for some time – in a friendship, a family, or at work – when you think that the other person should know better. Most people, including myself, are guilty of this, at some point, but anger is a natural response, in any case. Anger bursts in to occupy the space where one feels invisible, ignored – a chemistry of flame to show a presence of oxygen, unseen.

In this way, anger feels to me like grief: it rises to demonstrate a state of being there. I wonder if grief is now in my body and mind memory for the remainder of my life. As such, I may sometimes feel the connection, the crossover, the blurring of two emotional centers. Maybe to grieve is to accept that the quality of a person's life is the quality of one's emotional life, or that the quality of one's spiritual life navigates all of these. I can feel anger that is short-lived, a reminder of the soreness of grief; I am beginning to understand that the length of each – anger and grief -- is unconsciously determined and as mysterious as each individual.

March 16, 2013
Saturday

I wonder if I want my grief to end? In a way, it insulates me in its deep, emotional substance, from everything outside of it; even so, it is not as protective as that may sound. It seems to admit – even attract – other, more mundane, sources of stress. You could say that it almost ennobles stress, but it feels more complicated than that, day to day, in the experience of it.

The poignancy of grief is a path leading directly back to the loved one, a bone-deep sort of intimacy that is not only a comfort but an affirmation of love as the true indication of being fully alive.

Love applies itself to grief in order to alleviate it, and the point at which they meet is where my soul becomes conductive.

March 17, 2013
Sunday

After church this morning, I helped myself to the sliced apples and cheese that someone had brought for our coffee hour.

Such simple things can comfort your life, even order it. How many times in my life had someone prepared food for me? How many hands, through how many years, had sliced or spread or chopped or arranged items for me to eat, without my giving a thought to the intent and completeness of action that brought the food to my table, my plate?

I thought of my mother and of simple things like this that make me think of her. I feel a deep gratitude for all her preparations, her tasks, her intentions and perfect actions that were presented to me. May my deeply grateful heart cast back my love and thanks so as to cover all those years of your daily gifts, Mom – my young soul always knew them for what they were.

March 18, 2013
Monday

In grief, there is sharp pain and dull pain.

I feel sharp pain when I think of my mother in the hospital, out of her life, into the role of patient, and her suffering there; I know she hated all of it. I feel the dull pain on a daily level when I know that my visits to her today will all be in my mind. Then there are the pangs – when I reach for the phone or think of something I need to tell her, and, for a split second, all is as it was. I soften it all by sending loving thoughts to my mother in Heaven; I believe she receives them. If we could but rest there, the stress of grief could be diminished some. But the kinds of pain in grief come entirely from trying to reconcile or rebuild the past, and it is the lurching into the present that inspires the surge or rising of grief – one that will never expend itself, it would seem.

March 19, 2013
Tuesday

I went to a funeral the other day, and there were several eulogies given. The most meaningful, to me, was by the deceased man's cousin, who recalled memories of following his cousin around in the summer and the two of them fishing together; he was overcome, at times, in telling us about it. I could imagine the two boys together that summer, seventy years ago, and I was thankful to be sitting there, feeling a sense of his love for this man that I had known only slightly.

I began to think — what if that is a kind of treasure in grief — to know how deeply you can love, how ornate and intricate your responses, how long-lasting your devotion? It is a possession, this knowledge, and I explore it, however delicately, each moving day.

March 20, 2013
Wednesday

As I write the date out for this entry, I am thinking of how we recognize this first day of spring. To recognize means here to acknowledge, and not for the first time.

I couldn't tell you how I was feeling, if you asked me; there is absolutely no answer that arises in my mind. How *do* I feel? What is my emotional state, these days? My interior seems – feels? – completely neutral. It has no emotional articulation at all. Is this part of grief?

Do I recognize myself, in this manner of grief? I'm not sure; I know that grieving for my father was very different than for my mother. I can only think that each experience of grief must be its own incarnation, its own systems and movements. I don't know if we are supposed to recognize ourselves within it, and not for the first time.

March 21, 2013
Thursday

It is a lonely world without either of your
parents in it, no matter how many siblings or
friends you have. It's a particular kind of
loneliness, since a parent fills a role for you that
no one else does.

I miss my mother and father most at
dinnertime; the chill of an early spring evening
seems to come into my kitchen. I have lived
alone for years, but I have never felt more
alone at dinnertime than after my mother had
departed this world.

My parents loved dinnertime and would often
create the meal together. I remember the three
of us each evening raising our glasses of wine,
one of my father's own blends, in a toast
before we ate: "Sláinte!" "Cheers!" "Stin ugia
sas!" With those memories, something in me
settles for the night. I don't know that my body
or mind can ever truly incorporate the entire
loss of them.

March 22, 2013
Friday

Today, the family friend who cuts my hair said to me, "Your hair is just like your mother's! It grows fast and thick." It's a comfort to me to have my hair cut by the same person who cut hers, who also knew and loved her.

Grief understands place; it seems to settle into the place where it began – and it naturally can begin to be understood there, to be respected there, to be incrementally transformed into a living part of the ecosystem there, emotional and otherwise. If I go to places where we were, it's almost as if she is still here. I need that, because that place in time is where I still am.

March 23, 2013
Saturday

My friend René is recovering from a bone marrow transplant, now seventy-three days post- procedure. Each week, each day, has its challenges, some more difficult than others. He is navigating his recovery situation as best he can, and I know it is not easy for him: Lately, it resembles something like having a stomach flu for two and a half months (and counting). In and around this is his grief for his recently deceased mother; how to navigate that, in his recovery? Does it help or hinder his way back to health? In comparison, I started a new job in my most acute grieving months, and my days are hectic.

Each of us who grieves has to do so in the complexity of all the conditions of our lives, and everything has to keep moving along, in spite of it all. There is no one, pure life in stasis, in which to work through your grief, and it always feels as if you could do it better if you only had more time (and peace) in which to attend to it.

However, it could be that the rest of your life and all its conditions have to become part of your grief so that your grief, the newest element of you, becomes incorporated into who you are, as long as you live.

March 24, 2013
Sunday

Today is Palm Sunday. You went to church with me on several Palm Sundays, but the later years were different – I would save a palm frond for you, have Joanne make it into a cross before I left church, then present it to you when I got to your apartment soon after. You greatly treasured those palm crosses, and I found more than one when we cleaned out your place.

I miss my anticipation of seeing you after church, of telling you about the service, of giving you that palm cross. Those two hours of that Palm Sunday visit were two of the most precious hours of my year of our days, and our days, just the two of us together, were different than the calendar of our days with others. It is as if our calendar – our afternoons, our lunches, our visits to your doctors – were inside the other calendar and unknown by others.

I wore your favorite color today, purple, and I felt, at moments, that you stepped out of your time into mine.

Neither the present nor the past is entirely available to me.

March 25, 2013
Monday

Today was an ordinary Monday, until it snowed all morning, and we got dismissed at noon. The first greens of the flowers seemed stopped in their tracks – but that's only an illusion. Several of us ate lunch out and heard the thoughts that we don't have time to tell each other in any given week. Each one of us is such a complexity, such a bundle of stories.

I was thinking of what people saw when they looked at you – just a small, nicely dressed elderly woman. And all the time, you were so distinctive as a personality, were such a remarkable bundle of stories – some of the most intriguing I've ever heard. And all of them, our true heritage. You left me a great treasure in loving and knowing you and all your stories. And you infused them with yourself so much.

I want you to know that I remember them, and that I will carry both of us forward in them. Somewhere, then, here in this world, we will always be together.

March 26, 2013
Tuesday

I come to the late evening and realize that I
have missed my ritual of prayer today, which I
usually do right before dinner. I went out to
dinner and so forgot.

I pray for healing – for myself and several
others; I pray for those I love who are on the
other side of the veil of life, and I send love to
my parents and my niece, especially, there. This
prayer is a state something like meditation, but
not. These moments are units of time unlike
our minutes here, increments of something
measurable, in a substance that feels like love,
in its most peaceful state. Although to grieve is
to know you are different from what you were,
it still feels immovable.

Even so, as my mind rises from deep prayer, I
know I am changed.

March 27, 2013
Wednesday

Another cold spring day in the winter that seems never to end. It's odd that Holy Week and Easter are here, and I'm still wearing my winter coat. I am also resisting the holiday's arrival because I'm thinking, how can it be Easter without *you*?

You so enjoyed going to church with us, the spring flowers we'd bring you, our lunch together afterward. When we were young, you got each of us a homemade chocolate egg with our name in candy lettering on top, and I had seldom seen anything so pretty just for me. Thank you for the joy and reverence you brought to Easter and other holidays; they have retained that for me ever since.

Celebrating a holiday with a loved one generates a kind of emotional light within that holiday. You were our destination every Easter, the center of our celebration. Now, in everything I do for this holiday, love itself must be the center, and because of you, I know what that feels like.

March 28, 2013
Thursday

Today is Maundy Thursday, and I attended a service this evening. In such situations – at the most reverent moments – you often had something funny to say, a quirky observation that made every occasion with you so intimate. After the foot washing ceremony, I knelt to pray and send love to you and Dad, seeking the warm affection we three had for one another.

As I walked back to my pew, my bare feet on the cold bricks, I thought – you must have washed my feet when I was a baby, an occasion as intimate and profound. Grief is something remarkable in that it connects us to instances under time, through water, making us feel as delicate and vulnerable as babies, and as dependent on the love that steadies us every day. Grief seems to celebrate the ordinary, because that is where our love for our departed one was present every day; when I feel that for you, it is a relief to be, finally, so young, so delicate again.

March 29, 2013
Good Friday

The day started out well – exercising, checking
email, a hearty breakfast – but in church, I sank
into the story of the Passion deeply. At its end,
something nudged me to go up to the cross for
veneration. I knelt and touched the foot of the
cross, first with one hand's fingers, then the
other. I then began to weep. I got up and
walked back to my seat, still crying. At the end
of the service, some twenty minutes later, I
wanted to submerge myself in prayer, into the
peace of the marble floor beneath me.

I thought of Mary holding Christ's body, down
from the cross. What was the garden of Mary's
grief? If it came with the light of her son, who
tended *her* secret sorrow?

March 30, 2013
Saturday

Sometimes, when I am alone and engaged in something, it feels like grief *working*. I feel as if I am creating, over these many months, a new tool – a lens – by which to focus and move somewhere forward. I have been hammering out this new lens so that it fits my view perfectly, and if grief is this lens, I will find some sense of purpose in putting it to use.

It is a vast galaxy, the psyche, and I am only beginning to explore it, with my new tool.

March 31, 2013
Sunday

I find that one tendency in grief is to assume that whatever is going wrong that day would not have gone wrong if the loved one were still alive. Others may dismiss this reasoning, but it certainly feels true. I also find that grief depletes the coping reserves that would otherwise be available for the trials and tribulations of ordinary life. Yet grief also amplifies the profundity and depth of any beauty or joy one encounters, sometimes unexpectedly so.

Our Easter service came together in the trumpet, singing, and organ ensemble that seemed to echo the ages; we were roused – rightfully so – to remember that where there was misery there is still hope, in the world, and it offers us a particular kind of beauty, perhaps one that we might not have heard in the same way, if the loved one were alive.

April 1, 2013
Monday

In talking to one of my longtime friends today, I realized that experiencing grief offers friends a way to become closer – and not necessarily even talking about the grief itself. It's not depressing, at all – in fact, I feel a warm camaraderie, at such times, and we value each other (and maybe ourselves) even more. One thing my friend said was, "You begin to realize how many people are hurting in this world." And he is right. But eventually, like the hyacinths in my front yard, something breaks through, and a new growth pattern emerges.

There must be seasons inside of me, and my old friends can help me see the new season I am becoming.

April 2, 2013
Tuesday

I found Mom's checkbook today; it was nice to see her handwriting again. I know every instance for which she wrote each check, since I assisted in the ordinary day-to-day tasks of her life. I've had a cold for two weeks, and I know what remedies she would tell me to take and that she'd worry about its becoming an infection. The day-to-day intimacies of our lives are what most of us talk about every day, and I miss talking about ours. Tomorrow I fly to Savannah for a conference, and I'd like to hear her comments about that, just to make me feel more at home in the world, wherever I am.

Maybe they're right, those who say so: Maybe you are alive in my mind, as well as in Heaven, and you know I'm missing you and our calls every night at 7:15. I gaze out into the night as onto a river. It is 11:35.

April 3, 2013
Wednesday

I met a man in the airport today as we sat at a common eating area for lunch. He was in his seventies, and both his parents were still alive! He's lived nearly a whole lifetime without knowing the grief of losing a parent – remarkable, I thought. I envied him that, although his parents are in declining health (in their 90s), and he is responsible for their care. Even so, he can talk to them every day.

When I entered my hotel room this afternoon, I thought of my parents and our occasional stays in hotels on some vacations. How my mother loved all the toiletries they have for the guests and all the towels she didn't have to wash!

The goodness of our loved ones comes forward strongly in our memories, in mundane and satisfying ways. These memories fold into the mundane details of our current life and seem to be as if my parents are saying, "You can do this – you can continue your life, even though we are not there with you." It is hard to fathom this, but their message wanders in.

April 4, 2013
Thursday
Savannah, GA

There is a moment in my conversations with others when I have to decide whether or not to tell them about my mother's passing, if the topic would naturally come up. I often do not, but occasionally I do. People are kind, in such instances, and I'm never sorry that I mention it – even strangers can offer comfort. When I'm around no one but strangers for several days, as I am at this conference, I find that I need to tell at least one person, as if that grounds me, in some way. It is an instant connection of intimacy, and I find comfort in someone else's knowing that element of me while I'm here.

So am I never alone with my grief, after all?

April 5, 2013
Friday

I wonder if other grieving individuals feel as I do sometimes – as if my loved one's death were some sort of dream, as if I could imagine it away, or wake up from this life into my former one. I suspect others feel that, too. That could be why we so revere sleep, because, floating in the pre-conscious morning, all of life itself may as well be a dream. I felt something akin to that today when I was on the plane flying home – it seems so surreal to be moving through the middle of the air, and where is time, then? And where am I , when I traverse time?

Loving someone trails us back to reality – what was truly there then, and what is truly here now.

April 6, 2013
Saturday

Sometimes grief feels small – the small space in my day that she took up – a subtle look, a few words, a smile as a reply to a comment. But it is a place that remains empty, in the heart and at the table, in the room, in the doorway. No one can ever fill that space except the person who left because it was her very uniqueness that filled it. This is only a concept, until it is experienced in all its depth. And then, that one space in your life lingers with the air of what is missing – not empty, really, but held in honor, never forgotten, and never anything else than itself.

April 7, 2013
Sunday

I am thinking of my friend, Helen, who died suddenly five years ago today. I still miss her, and it was a singular gift to be her friend for fourteen years. Strangely, today I grabbed what I thought was my copy of *Great Expectations* to read for school this week, and when I opened it, I saw Helen's handwriting; it was her copy. Not only do I love reading her funny comments in the margins, but also it harkens back to a time in my life when I was happier, if only because Helen and my parents were all alive. I settle into the memory of those years like into a comfortable chair and leisurely read each page of mental scenes, of anecdotes, even the ambiance of those years and the quality of late afternoon sunlight in my old classroom whose tall, louvered windows never quite closed.

How much more do we get to learn about someone after they have died? And, more significant perhaps, how much more do we get to know about ourselves – or about love itself -- from loving that person?

April 8, 2013
Monday

It seems to me that, as a grieving person, I am either very aware of my emotions on any given day or completely unable to identify my emotional state at all. My therapist says that the latter condition is when the emotions shut down, due to fatigue, in order to regroup and regain their equilibrium. I agree, but it is a very strange state, and I would choose almost any emotion over the complete lack thereof. The unpredictable, comprehensive tides by which grief moves can surprise us, but they also seem as natural as the peace of an evening or the way we float away in sleep. Perhaps to suffer in grief is to fully accept it and know that its systems function as much with the natural world as anything else does.

Grief should never be set aside or apart, then, but waits for our acceptance; in truth, our bodies already know this, and accept it every day.

April 9, 2013
Tuesday

A ticking clock is like a beating heart: as much and as constant as anything in the atmosphere of your mind. And when the ticking clock stops – silence fills the air like a rushing wind. So, too, when a life stops, and the impact is to reorient silence so that its new form fits into your system. The most natural inclination is to stare out a window while your mind and all your faculties reassemble your inner atmosphere; we do this so that our home and our mind are balanced with nature's environment. Trees understand this silence; birds sit within it. The layers of earth are ordered by it.

A friend and former coworker of mine died last night; I'm sorry I didn't visit him when I learned he was sick some months ago. I couldn't seem to bring forth the energy to make that happen. My mind now reorders, reassembles, works to assimilate the new silence that I will never fully understand.

April 10, 2013
Wednesday

I have found that grieving seems to slow down my thinking, my responses to life, my emotions themselves. In that state, I feel, as if blindly, for something to pull me forward through the day, the week. All I want is a thin fiber of hope – something ahead of me that says "this may yet be possible." If I can finger that thin fiber in my mind, I can follow it to the world beyond my grief, my day, my silent house.

The hope comes from another part of my life, the part that still hears rain as something good and that interprets daily what numbered day of spring it is.

April 11, 2013
Thursday

I was nostalgic this evening for a time in my life that was professionally intense, socially rich, and intimate with friendships and colleagues whom I would come to cherish for decades afterward – my first teaching days in 1994. This capacity to cherish such periods and experiences has taken on another dimension lately, since I have experienced grief. It is as if I now have an entire mental department allocated for nostalgia, and my mind is busy assorting, organizing, arranging details for further study and for the ability to feel deeply about these memories in the future, like laying a path back to them so that they will have the greatest impact and depth of feeling when my mind next returns to them.

This nostalgia of place, of memory – a personality, an occasion, a friendship's beginning – reminds me that peace and goodness are natural; they are comforting in ways unique to each individual, whose emotional temperament fires through hundreds of complexities. How complex, then, is grief, and what comes forth in my system to recognize it, grow to it, bring it into what I am? Grief, which feels so distinct from a life without it, is spun entirely from one's own organic components, emotionally, and I can only marvel at that, and be grateful.

April 12, 2013
Friday

One thing I never expected to happen as I grieved was to gain weight; I've gained nearly ten pounds in these past ten months. Mostly, I wanted to feel connected to an ordinary and simple pleasure in life, deciding not to restrict my diet and thereby miss some food I might enjoy. Or maybe I just didn't care anymore.

The scent of particular foods, the tasting, chewing, swallowing – it is all a very intimate experience of your body's interacting with the world, and if my mind could not do that, maybe I just wanted my body to do so. I love the precious world and my body all the more for it.

April 13, 2013
Saturday

At this date, my mother has been gone ten months. Part of me wants to remain here, or slow time such that it almost does not move. Each day that passes is further from my mother, and, gradually, less and less of her will filter into my day. Yesterday, I found a change purse that was hers; I thought about saving the two pennies and one nickel that were in it. (I put them in a box of other coins.) I am using that little purse now. I can still hear her voice in my mind, when she said, every night, after I said I loved her and good night: "I love you, too, sweetheart."

When my mother was sick in the hospital, the most frequent comment that greeted me each day from the nurse on duty was, *Are you Betsy? She's been asking for you.* The last day my mother was fully conscious, she had the nurse call me after I had returned home (she was not awake during my visit that afternoon). When the nurse held up the phone to my mother, she said to me, very weakly, "I love you." It was all she could get out. I was amazed that she was awake and had been able to communicate with the nurse enough to call me. "I love you, Mummy," I said, using the term of endearment I had chosen years before because it was what she called her own mother. I was on my deck, in the warm light of an early June evening; the water in my bird bath seemed luminous. She was giving me that message with her last strength, and I was humbled and overwhelmed; it was one of the greatest gifts of my life, those four minutes.

That light, on that evening, remains out of time and carries her love to me still.

April 14, 2013
Sunday

I attended the viewing of an old friend and former co-worker this evening. A few others were also there, sitting around chatting, and an argument ensued, at one point, about visiting the friend of ours who is currently recovering from a bone marrow transplant. There were hurt feelings after the argument, and one person left abruptly. Another was very affected by talking to the widow and her children, and was then edgy and teary. There seemed to be such emotional entropy stirred up – sadness, anxiety, numbness, anger, impatience, irritability. And behind all this was the deceased's body lying in the casket, as well as all the photos of his life on the wall.

Walking up to the casket, I felt sadness but felt also the peace that settles on you, if you allow it, and are still within yourself. If all viewings were silent, that stillness would be a balm.

April 15, 2013
Monday

Today at the Boston Marathon there were bombings on the sidewalk by the finish line. Reports say that two people died, and one hundred more were wounded, some critically. The authorities are not yet sure which terrorists are responsible. I was dazed by the tragedy of the news. My first response was to call my mother and get her reaction; it seems so inconceivable that I cannot. I always felt unsettled until I spoke to her, in such shocking events as these, as if I were floating around until she caught hold of me, balancing me out, emotionally.

My mother was very intelligent, and I appreciated her perspective on things. In her absence, no one balances me out, and I just drift. I'm weary, and there is no closure.

The day simply ends.

April 16, 2013
Tuesday

The toll is now three dead, 186 wounded in Boston. One man who had lost both his sons – to suicide and to war – was watching the race and ran to help another man whose legs were severely wounded in the blast. The man who assisted was grateful for the opportunity to help, he said. I'm wondering: Does grief make one a better person?

I think it can, if you allow it. But you must be willing to let parts of you fall away, without knowing what those are. Something else slowly forms, like a mist, that you step into, until you only know you have changed because sometimes you can see through the blur of daily life into the stillness beneath it and see into others. Then, as you listen to someone speak of a problem, you wait attentively until whatever their stillness is becomes words; grief has taught you to hear and see what is before and under words, and if you can understand or empathize into that stream of layered language, you are the better for it, that day.

April 17, 2013
Wednesday

The people I work with have only known me,
for the most part, since I have been in grief.
Whom are they seeing? What version of me are
they getting to know? I feel sometimes as if I
am shimmering behind a curtain, and it might
be to protect me while I am becoming
whomever I am becoming. My day-to-day life is
almost beside the point.

I see everything from a great distance, over a
huge vista, and I watch the clouds along the
horizon. When I adjust back to the present
moment and its demands, I am sometimes
resentful in having to do so. My new colleagues
must see this distance within me. Maybe they
realize that, once established, it is impossible to
separate the grief, settling like fog in the valley
of the psyche, from the person they know.

April 18, 2013
Thursday

Today I met Rita Dove, former U.S. Poet Laureate and author of nine volumes of poetry and other books. I have been teaching her poems for twenty years; she is as normal and natural as anyone could wish a famous poet to be. I asked her about how to choose a publisher for a finished poetry manuscript, and she said the old rules still are good to go by – seeing what kinds of poetry each house publishes.

The gift for me today is in reliving the time when I first saw an interview of Rita Dove with Bill Moyer on television all those years ago and subsequently decided to teach her poems. Those memories offer a chance to remind myself of my actual center, distant from time, space, family, only because the center is spiritual and therefore out of time. It is one of the greatest gifts of writing poetry – writing into the center of time, of identity, until you arrive at the truest definition of yourself, creating. It is from a moment of this perspective that I saw myself this evening, out of circumstance, watching a new Earth and life move around me, knowing I am still in the flux of life but feeling a still kind of freedom that connects me to myself at any year of my life.

If grief makes you see into eternity from a dark precipice, it is also fertile ground for repositioning yourself in the timeline of your life, to feel your own unique stability.

April 19, 2013
Friday

Each evening, day, afternoon, I feel a little less secure in the world, the world of my own life, since neither of my parents is in it anymore. When I went out in the evening, I knew my mother would want to be sure that I returned home safely; no amount of solicitous care from anyone else can take the place of that secure backdrop that is a parent in one's life.

At the same time, grief can cause a dulling of the anxieties, such that it does not much seem to matter what one does; the end will be absence and loss, so the immediate and daily concerns of life fall away. Somehow, never suspecting either of these extremes – complete security or a lack of caring about one's safety -- I lived my previous life floating somewhere within this huge realm, not discerning that there were boundaries, or that those I loved so deeply held those boundaries for me.

Now life expands out into all of space itself, and somehow I must begin to feel as if I belong.

April 20, 2013
Saturday

I must be in a different stage of my grief and healing now because today I could tell a stranger at Weight Watchers why I had gained the weight I have over the last ten months – grief over my mother's passing. I explained to her that I turned to food because I wanted *one* thing to feel good every day, and food is 100% dependable for that. She expressed sympathy over my loss, and I accepted it. It feels good to be back on Weight Watchers and therefore be in control of my eating, exercise, and nutrition. Grief stresses all levels – emotional, mental, and physical.

As for the spiritual part of me, I know that it has needs – a peaceful relationship with God, regular prayer, regular worship -- but I do not think grief stresses it as much as it sends a long resounding note through its depths and caverns. That note opens the spiritual dimension within you, where profound sadness meets the eternal, like someone standing on a cliff in the moonlight. Strangely, we intuit that we are very near another country because there seems a ribbon of light that the loved one sends back to us in the space between the precipice and the night air. It is very difficult to know when to walk back home.

April 21, 2013
Sunday

I keep a photo of my mother on a bookcase in my living room, a fairly recent photo of her sitting in a chair outdoors, looking directly at the camera. I talk to her, in this photo, every morning, afternoon, and evening. I can still hear the sound of her voice in my head, which can be comforting. I wish I had a picture of the two of us together, but I will make do with this one.

I keep it there not just to talk to, but so that something outside of my head reflects what is so much in it. This is especially true if someone comes into my home who never knew my mother. It is not unlike hanging a framed diploma on the wall of an office. "This is what I am made of, what degree I have earned; these are my credentials in achieving some level of a compassionate citizen, of a loving daughter, one whose past currently feels so much more substantive than her present." The photo of my mother holds a space where my past does not have to end, and my present will never exist.

April 22, 2013
Monday

I received some good news about a job today, and I could not wait to tell my mother, whom I felt had been hoping for this with me, all along. At first, I was reminded that I could not call her, so experienced sadness and disappointment; the pleasure of telling her would have been nearly equal to receiving the news myself. But it then occurred to me that perhaps this awareness of her sharing my life never has to end. If she loves me still, from where she is now, and I believe she does, then she likely knows the good news I have received and is happy for me. It's not the same as surprising her with the news myself, but it's a comfort.

Grief is the place that navigates the other realm with our earthly one, and this territory is new to most of us. This new territory is like a causeway between countries, and it is just as important that ordinary day-to-day events be communicated within it as it is heavy, life-changing ones. Both are equally profound here, because in the intimacy of the ordinary, it is actually the transport of love.

April 23, 2013
Tuesday

I was wondering today how many dimensions of grief exist within one person, and if the outer layers are in some way permeable. I can remember feeling as I felt several months ago, although the organic nature of grief – and it is of nature – is such that one never feels the same way two days in a row. But the layers nearest the air and other people could be affected not merely by grief itself but also by my encounters with everything in the environment around me.

What if I grieved very differently than I otherwise would have, these last seven months, because of where I worked? The people I met and came to know? Where does the person end and the grief begin?

April 24, 2013
Wednesday

I find, in living alone, that I must create my own boundaries for my emotions, thoughts, and perceptions in my own home, each day. I watch the spring dusk, the delicate green coming forth, and my grief goes into it as if into an embrace. Where does this green, this immersion into the new foliage, blend with my thoughts? I seem to sleep into it, think within it, and I watch the birds come to my bird bath as if they are bringing something to me.

Sometimes I lapse into the soft daze of a long-lived grief, a companion that almost stands in for the companionship of my mother. It is a kind of company, a presence in my house, when the world outside is so busy, coming to life.

April 25, 2013
Thursday

I think that there always will be days when the grief for my mother will rise into a moment of my day, then fall back, enough to remind me that the empty darkness in my mind that is grief's territory is vast, yet immediately accessible. This occurred when, in prayer, I asked her to be with me at my poetry reading at the college this evening; since she had been with me at the college before, the deep sadness at missing her was acute. However, I do believe that both she and my father were present, in whatever dimension they could be, and my reading went well.

When I drove the forty-four miles home, I sought them in the territory of my mind that is filled with their memories and my loss; the entrance there is crowded with words, but once inside, in the dim silence, I seek only their faces and the love that crosses our space.

April 26, 2013
Friday

As I feel one phase of my life, this job, coming to a close, and another phase beginning, I experience anxiety, which puzzles me. I don't know that I rise to joyfulness as readily as I once did, and I'm not sure that I will ever go back to that kind of ease again.

Traveling through the experience of grief, I sometimes feel anxiety, with two results: I'm not sure where it comes from or why I'm feeling it, and I am not sure I will be able to resolve it. The fact that it may be natural or understandable is really little help, since it does nothing to mitigate the feeling. Prayer connects me to God and is healing, yet it takes practice to clarify that connection to the divine. When grief demonstrates the depth and power of new things in your life, anything new that follows in its wake carries with it the same sound of rushing waters, and part of me would simply like to drift away, and let the waves redesign me.

April 27, 2013
Saturday

Things end all the time.

Classes end, semesters end, jobs end, associations end, and we deal with it smoothly or unconsciously or haltingly. But new phases are constantly beginning. This afternoon, I was driving down the highway and began weeping at a Beach Boys song. I usually played that cd when I went to pick up my mother every Saturday evening for dinner out. I felt the sharp loss of her, and I wept. It can happen for no reason or for a good reason, but it can rise into your consciousness as acutely sharp and empty as in the first week of grief. All of these things are embedded in our psyche – near or far – and they are not intruders there. They are entirely our own, and they have a right to their own rising and falling.

April 28, 2013
Sunday

Grief feels familiar, in a way. I think it is akin to every experience of loneliness. I considered some significant beginnings of that in my life, such as being abruptly separated from my twin sister when we started kindergarten. In Delaware public schools, in the 1960s, twins were not permitted to be in the same class or to see each other during the day, including even at lunchtime and recess. On our first day of kindergarten, two different teachers came down the hall toward us; each took one of us by the hand and pulled us in opposite directions. We were appalled and afraid and began crying. I suddenly knew that the adults did not comprehend the enormity of what they were doing. My teacher was young, blond, and pleasant. When she put cookies and milk on each desk, I could barely swallow any of it. Later, I asked to go to the bathroom so that I could walk down the long hallway to stand outside my sister's classroom door (I saw where they took her); I recognized the sound of her weeping, on the other side. I stood there for some time.

Loneliness was part of the anxiety I felt when my mother went out in the evening when I was a young child, the mother who best understood the bond I had with my sister; loneliness arises with emptiness in a relationship, or in a new place, alone. It is all grief.

No matter how much company you have or what company you keep, grief creates a kind of unique loneliness, designed in detail by the person who is gone. In their wake, loneliness knows exactly how to find us, because there is already a place – an old place – for it within us. And we know exactly how it feels.

April 29, 2013
Monday

Because each human being is unique, the way
we love each person is unique; you don't love
any two people the same way. Yesterday, I
defined grief as a form of loneliness, but there
is also a sense of kinship in the experience. The
closest "kin" are those who knew and loved
your loved one. You all understand and know
that person and what was required to love him
or her. On a larger scale, there is a kinship of all
who lost their mother, or all who lost a parent,
or simply all who lost someone they loved
deeply.

This is what the trees have been whispering all
along – leaves rustle in the evening air, leaves
are falling, life is falling; *listen*, they seem to
say. This air of knowledge, this intimate
message, floats past our faces in busy times
and calm times, and we usually ignore it against
our cheek. But in a glance, a moment we
choose, we turn toward it and feel it open, with
our love for someone, into the whole sky, as if
it were an ocean of time itself. We know it is
the juncture of time and eternity, and, finally,
we feel at home, standing on the damp earth
under the gazing moon.

April 30, 2013
Tuesday

Today I learned that my friend's partner died suddenly, at home, probably from a heart attack. This was very sad and shocking news; I'd visited with them on many occasions, together on their deck, or in my house, or out to dinner; we three had a deep connection. He was a dear man, and we shared a common interest in literature and writing. The world is now a worse place, an emptier place, a less hopeful place. My friend will be in a grieving state for months, possibly years, and she will never have the same kind of life again. One life ended changes many lives.

He turns now, in spirit, to his new existence. And we here are left to watch the moving system, the deciduous days.

May 1, 2013
Wednesday

Sometimes I worry that, at some point, I won't be able to imagine my mother's face, with all her familiar expressions. I do not want my only visions of her face to be the ones in photographs.

Do we look at people in ways particular to them, particular for that person? If feels so, to me. I try to remember how she looked at me, and where we went, and what we talked about. I drive around those same places now, turn the same corners, see the same trees, and remember that I had another life then, and that it was, in fact, a completely different place.

May 2, 2013
Thursday

My friend, Carolyn, who just lost her partner
suddenly, has eleven brothers and sisters. And
not one of them will be able to make her feel
less alone, less deeply alone, in certain
moments. Her most intimate and loving
comfort can only come from where her love for
John meets the emptiness of time, at the
border between life and the afterlife.

She can imagine him sending and receiving
love, imagine hearing his voice. In order to hear
that best, she wants the whole world silent —
because, I suspect, the roaring in her ears will
not stop.

May 3, 2013
Friday

Because it is now May, my mother seems more immediately gone. Last May was the last time she was well and inside her ordinary life, so it seems as if I could drive over to Forwood Manor and visit her there. I would see her in the lobby, probably with Ruth, and then we would go up to her apartment and visit, or I'd tend to things she needed help with. At Forwood, in May, the pink azaleas would be in bloom and the purple and yellow pansies arranged in orderly rows out front. As I walked to the large front doors, I'd hear the flag whipping high up against the flag pole and watch a crow or two fly up to the roof. I miss that outside world that was part of my life with her; when I walked in or out of Forwood Manor, it was as if there was someone aware of it all with me, at the time.

Love gives the whole world a personality, and I wish I could go back in time and talk to it then, whatever was watching me, before I went through the door.

May 4, 2013
Saturday

Today was comprised of three significant visits. The first was a wedding shower, and there were touching moments of deep sentiment from mother to daughter. I also loved the hostess's pets: two turtles and two dogs.

The second was a visit to my neighbor and friend whose partner died suddenly on Monday. I sat with her for about an hour and a half; I listened and consoled, as best I could. The whole world has shifted, and I could feel that in her. It was a privilege to be there with Carolyn.

The third was a visit to my friend René, recovering from his bone marrow transplant. We went to dinner, then returned to his apartment and watched a movie, "Mildred Price," with Joan Crawford.

What do I feel as I walk through these lives? Astounded – that I am witness to such deep love in the world, that I can take part in such deep friendship, that there are so many intricate emotional ecosystems within people. I am beginning to think everything connects to that ecosystem – including one's physical, mental, and spiritual selves. I wonder what combination, what systems, anyone sees in us, on any given day?

May 5, 2013
Sunday

Grief has taught me to say what needs to be said – at least, I try to do this most of the time. This includes loving, as well as more mundane, comments, but all can be constructive. Each of us just muddles through life, as best we can, and thoughtful words can help, if they are honest and respectful. Love helps us understand each other better.

I miss you, Mom, because you understood me completely, and your greatest gift was to remind me that I was loved, entirely. However you said that, I understood you.

May 6, 2013
Monday

Emily Dickinson wrote, "After great pain, / a formal feeling comes." I think of this as I listen to my friend tell me of the plans for the service for her partner who died last week.

But this formal feeling that helps in planning a service is not actually *after* pain – the pain does not recede, exactly. It is as if the pain is a great wave that heaves you onto a certain level – a sand bar – that allows you to move dazedly through the necessary decisions of planning a service. It is some time later when the tide slowly rises and lifts you back into the water; this is an element you will begin to live under, that slows sound and muffles the harsh busyness of day-to-day life, until one day – if you can call such measurements days – the great waters recede, and you are standing in your own town, and all appears in a different season. Grief has moved from water to foliage, shadow, and breeze. I feel these now, and I watch the birds fly through them, fluidly.

May 7, 20913
Tuesday

I hear the rain falling on this spring night, and I'm not sure why it seems sad and lively at the same time. Rain dampens down your thoughts that rise elsewhere, beyond time, into memories, and it reminds you: *You are here!* – You exist here, where it is raining, and where all of spring's creatures and greenery are growing around you.

When we share a memory of another person, reminiscing together, something brightens that memory within us, and that small point of love's reflection reminds us what the center of our being is. We know we grieve because we love, and we love because that is our substance, especially here.

May 8, 2013
Wednesday

Mother's Day is approaching, and I find myself turning off the stimuli that come toward us – through every form of media – since I don't really know how to respond to this day. It doesn't feel solemn, really, nor emotionally wrenching when I think about it. Mostly, it feels like something I am far removed from, although this evening I found myself staring at the yellow mug I gave you last Mother's Day. I feel more resistant than sad. Can you celebrate Mother's Day on your side, Mom, even though your children are all over here? We will think of you with love, on Sunday, and we join all those who look away into a distance under the close and mothering sky.

May 9, 2013
Thursday

Every ordinary day can seem to have no particular meaning at all, except to make one feel more weary than the day before. But there are unexpected points in the day that rise above this, in the heart, and you realize that the day is simply an open field on which anything can happen – each day gives open space, and time, to the increments of life.

Today, watching a girls' lacrosse game, I recognized a girl I know, across the field. I texted her, and I saw her reach for her phone; she texted me back. That encounter, in its friendly intimacy, was the best in my day, my own field that grief has nourished so thoroughly.

May 10, 2013
Friday

In missing my mother today, I had the thought:
The intimacy you have with any one person can
never be fulfilled by another person. Each
relationship gives you sustenance in a form that
cannot be realized with any other relationship,
so when a loved one dies, that need cannot be
filled ever again in that same way.

So when someone says, "Well, you have other
children to love," or "You'll find someone else,"
that kind of aphorism seems not just clueless
and insensitive but almost cruel in its
dismissiveness. Since the loss of a mother
prompts no such comments and is, I would say,
universally understood as unlike any other kind
of loss, I don't have to think of any response to
others' comments besides, "thank you." But
every loss is like no other, and one can only
wait for the fertile heart, in its own season, to
love something, someone, in another beginning
– in respect to all the relationships that have
gone before it.

May 11, 2013
Saturday

Every one you have known has a memory of you in certain years or segments of your life; this is one of the reasons that relationships are so valuable. And you retain others' history, as well. When I watched five of my students graduate from college today, they walked across the stage with four years of my life, too. My mother was in those years, so they knew me as an active daughter and caregiver.

These days, instead of deep sadness, I think I feel my mother around as if she were on the other side of a glass door, looking in at me, smiling. She is in my world, but not my day.

May 12, 2013
Sunday

Today is Mother's Day, and I felt a range of emotions throughout it, but, to my surprise, the dominant feeling for me was – bewilderment. Although my mother has been gone for almost eleven months, I am still at times bewildered by her absence. I spoke to a friend of mine today, who also lost his mother in the last year, and we both seemed a bit lost, ourselves.

While your mother is alive, you are still in a womb in the world; once she is gone, you are born into a second life, disconnected in the most profound way. This new world seems sometimes without substance – or it could be we who seem so. Cell by cell, you come back into being and eventually look around, surprised at realizing you are still here, not entirely recognizing whatever you are.

May 13, 2013
Monday

It is now exactly eleven months since my mother departed this world. I make an effort every day to remember the sound of her voice and things she would say. I want her presence in my mind to be alive, not anything like a recording, playing over and over again. If I am tired, as I often seem to be these days, I can drift in and out of reality, so to speak, and feel as if I am walking back and forth between a calm dream and my normal life. Both have the memory of my mother; I prefer the realm of dreams and a dreamy mid-day state, but it was the ordinary day where my mother and I interacted and lived.

All the ordinary, mundane days she walked through tell me – if they were good enough for her, who am I to choose?

May 14, 2013
Tuesday

Since my mother left us, my vague tolerance of endings seems to have left with her. Endings drop things – relationships, daily conversations, nearness, an accustomed space you inhabit. Endings make you look back and evaluate middles and beginnings. Endings precipitate loss. And a new beginning may yet be very far off.

Nothing organic is solid – including a life; it all dissolves, expires, stops turning. The reserves that are called forth to navigate endings dwindle. I even wrestle with the ending of a day. If I'm so tired, why can't I just stop, lie down, and turn off the light? Something in me has already done so.

May 15, 2013
Wednesday

There comes a time in the life of every grieving person when the loved one can be described as having *died*, rather than having *passed away*. Sometimes the declaration flows in and out of those two phrases, and "died" never feels right. People say "passed away" because it is softer than "died," and at first you just can't bring yourself to say "died." I still edge away from that word, which sounds bald and impersonal. Words are like a bridge you walk over. I don't want anyone hearing my footsteps when they clatter on the bridge: *She's gone. She's gone. She's gone.* How can that be?

Surely, it was just a few days ago when I made a cup of tea in her kitchen and brought it into the living room to chat with her. No wonder these words we choose matter so much – they have to carry time and meaning and love over a great space. My mother passed away eleven months and two days ago.

May 16, 2013
Thursday

Tim, Carolyn's partner's son, contacted me today for advice and suggestions about his father's celebration-of-life service. He had lined up speakers, planned music, prepared photos for display. My thoughts went to my father's and mother's services, both of which I planned with my siblings; such ceremonies are an important thing to focus on and serve as a way to show respect to the deceased. I tried to convey to the son today to incorporate silence, rest, into the ceremony, to choose a few speakers over many, a few good remembrances as more effective than a dozen.

No one cares much about thoughts and words, at such occasions; true, deep sentiment holds sway, and it can fill a room, beyond all faces, all photographs, all music. Each of us settles in and rests in that dark stillness, for a moment, with our own woes and memories of loved ones gone. Every service is a comfort to us all.

May 17, 2013
Friday

Every life is imperfect, so every grief is imperfect. Because of a lack of time, I have missed or neglected calling, writing, or mourning people I would have liked to. I grieve for my loved ones lost and wonder if I could be handling it better. Am I grieving too much? Not enough? In the right stages? Do I even know how I am feeling, from day to day? Am I thinking of my mother in the way that is best for my grief? The best spiritual way? The best way that respects our relationship?

Since every grief experience is its own entity, as unique as each relationship, there's either no simple answer, or the answer could be forming for years. We live with the life we have, from day to day, and every life has frustration. Love holds lives together, and grief is as adaptable and as accepting of life's imperfections as any of us needs it to be.

May 18, 2013
Saturday

Today I took part in a remembrance ceremony
for John, speaking about his relationship with
his partner, Carolyn. I also read my sonnet,
"The Heron," which John liked very much. I was
near tears at two points in my talk, but it did
not bother me; there was also quiet laughter
from the audience at several parts of my
comments, which I intended and appreciated.

During the service I was thinking that his loved
ones are just beginning to feel the tip of grief –
like looking at a part of the night sky with a
telescope – and that some of them may
gradually become aware that grief itself
actually expands into the whole sky. Eventually,
this true darkness, this expanse of love, is
something one can rest within and feel almost
welcomed by.

The Heron
for W.S.

The heron's eyes are nothing like the sun;
the greying sky less somber than her head.
The blue of her Great Blue could be outdone;
If feathers, words, hers may go unread.
I have seen ospreys, hawks more deftly fly,
but no slow spirals from this narrow bird;
and egrets seem to know more how to lie
on air that lifts and falls to move them forward.

I love to see her soar, yet there is talk
That others climb the sky with clearer purpose.
I grant I never saw a symbol walk;
my heron's feet hold firm to muddy surface.
And yet, by morning tides and shifting sands,
the heron turns the sky, and nothing of her
    lands.

May 19, 2013
Sunday

When I look at the picture of my mother before which I stop every day, I feel as if she knows what is going on in my life now, whether because I have said so to this picture every evening or whether because of her awareness, wherever she is, I don't know. I only know that it matters to me that she is still part of my life, today. I do not believe that I will ever feel differently.

On Friday, I felt a momentary happiness when I suddenly intuited her presence in the room – a brief visit – as real as if she had just walked through the door. Her message: She "met" John, my neighbor's deceased partner, in her realm and enjoyed seeing him again (they had met before at my house). Then I was alone again. Who of us can know entirely what presence of person or love floats in or away from our consciousness?

May 20, 2013
Monday

When I heard the birds singing and chattering on this mild spring evening at dusk, I felt a kinship with my late father.

Listening to birdsong at the close of day always reminds me of my father. He and I shared a love of birds; he could identify them not only on sight but also by their call. It's a sweet kind of sadness, this memory, but I would not give it up for anything. It is nine and a half years since he passed away, and I miss him still.

What does a person do with the frustration of missing someone? Where to direct that energy that stretches after the loved one? It seems to exist, this energy, as if it were a living element. And so much of ourselves do we pour into it, sometimes feeling more alive in that connecting tunnel of energy, that it can feel as if we do not entirely belong outside of it. If nothing else, grief teaches patience; sometimes there is nothing productive to do but wait, to see what else shifts within that tunnel.

May 21, 2013
Tuesday

Sunday was Pentecost, so yesterday began my favorite time of the church calendar year: Ordinary Time. This is as if the other, more dramatic, times of the liturgical year are taking a light nap – so all of the depth and complexity and beauty of the thousand whirring details not only of our faith but of life – and of our lives – can gradually float around and up for us to study, ponder, sift through. Each day has a myriad of thoughts, sensations, emotive moments – and Ordinary Time, encouraged in faith, allows the calm and undisturbed environment for the profound and simple contemplations in life.

Experiences of loss and grief require time and attention so that you can take each small piece, shape it to yourself, then place it within, on your own shelf; this occurs silently and mysteriously – and from our perspective, imperfectly. And, of course, by imperfect we mean in an ordinary day, with all the small gifts that rise within it.

May 22, 2013
Wednesday

I know spring is supposed to be a time of initiating life, of burgeoning flowers and foliage, and of renewed energy, but I feel more tired and emotionally weary each morning than I did the morning before. I also know that this form of burn-out is a complex weaving of threads from the job I am leaving and the grief I have been moving through in the past year. I find it difficult to sustain a focus in the classroom each day and to put my shoulder behind the plow of all the daily tasks and demands this job requires.

My mother would understand, I think to myself, yet she has never met any of these people I spend my day with, every weekday. But she always made an effort to listen to the details of my day, and we could always look forward to doing something together that week. Such a simple balance to one's day seems as natural and inevitable as the breeze or sunlight, but once gone, you have to try to right yourself every given day, and I am as weary as if I have created every day from scratch.

May 23, 2013
Thursday

If grief is the ultimate experience of loss, in life, I wonder if I am better or worse at it for having experienced other forms of loss before?

Today I announced to my students that I would not be returning next year, and we all felt the initial sting of losing each other's company in the months to come. And what can I tell them about the subject? That navigating loss, change, and transition gets easier? That it becomes less difficult to create new situations, new homes, new relationships? It doesn't, necessarily, although one does acquire the confidence that one can survive life's changes without feeling despondent and lost indefinitely. And I suppose I should address myself in grief as I would in any other experience of loss and transition: It takes time – there's an unknowable process to it – but you will get through it and find you have other things to contribute in this world, this world that needs your new self and what you bring with you, as no one else in the same way can.

May 24, 2013
Friday

When you are a primary caregiver, there are good days and bad days – when the loved one is fickle and irritable or funny and friendly. There are days when you are driven to anger and frustration beyond rational thought or when the best part of your day is seeing her at the door when you pick her up. There are days when you cannot wait to get away from each other, and days when that person's presence was all the company you needed that day. Those complexities that comprise a relationship do not mitigate the love at all; they just require navigating through them, as they occur.

Is it inevitable to be harsh with yourself later, for what you should have said or done differently? Yes; many people who were caregivers have told me so. But grief reminds you what is real in life and in relationships. And as a former caregiver of many years, I know every day and hour of grief I have felt underscores the reason I cared for my mother in the first place – I loved her all my life and still do.

May 25, 2013
Saturday

My sister flew to New Hampshire today to help with the birth of her twin grandsons, and I walked away from a part of my life I am finishing up, professionally. Each such occasion shifts the world. I have detached emotionally, on several levels, and I am looking forward to a summer of peace.

Sometimes a period of peace – an hour, a day, a season – is all that a grieving person hopes for. Since grief feels as if it expands into every cell of your being, it is sometimes difficult to imagine that you can ever again feel the smooth serenity of peace. I am not sure if we can ever achieve it fully, but glimpses come, eventually, and we can remember that peace is not always achieved alone. Standing on my deck, watching the breeze-tossed leaves, birds busily completing their tasks, the scent of damp soil drifting by, the moody clouds of spring coming into view – peace accepts all these ingredients and encloses grief with their friendly company; we who hold the still space within that are grateful.

May 26, 2013
Sunday

"It's very hard," my friend said, of her life now without her partner. "Yes, it's a new life, which you have to create, bit by bit," I said. I wish I could say more, but a grieving person needs the truth, needs and deserves for us not to arbitrate their pain. And sometimes they do not need you to say anything; just for you to be there is a comfort to them.

You can see profound love -- as if it is a secret person -- turning toward you in every grieving face: the luminous brown of eyes, the poignant expression, the love like a pool of water in a face – like no other expression I've ever seen, and have never forgotten, once witnessed.

May 27, 2013
Monday

Today is Memorial Day, and on television I watched the veterans of World War II visit the war memorials in Washington, D.C.. Their stoic grief is many decades old, so they handle it with grace, but it is no less real or deep to them, these many years later. The depth of their selfless sacrifice radiates from them, even though they are humble in speech and demeanor. It is they whom we are there to witness, as much as we are there to witness those who weep so openly as they touch the names engraved on memorials.

It all goes straight down to the center of life, around which every day, every face, every relationship turns and grief exalts – love established, breathing, living, holding forth, standing witness.

May 28, 2013
Tuesday

If I could write a letter: *Dear Mom – Thanks for dropping in to visit, at times; it's wonderful to feel your presence. I wish we could have a conversation; I would like to look forward to going to lunch with you, to going to Gabrielle's graduation party with you, to hearing your concern about Chris's eye surgeries. You would not believe how they've expanded the Hollywood Grill, Mom – there's no counter where we sat and ate lunch so many times. I can see you sitting there now, eating your lentil soup, sharing a grilled cheese with me, and talking to whatever stranger was sitting next to you, as was your habit. (They seemed often to brighten at the attention from you, always so curious about people.)*

How do I navigate a relationship with my mother now? Do we create a new relationship with our loved one, now gone? How does grief weave a new relationship between the one we had and the one we need and want in the present? "There is magic in the web of it," Othello says, of his mother's handkerchief and its mysterious creation. The magic is the love between us while we both live; it is eternal and spins a transference, a living element, between us. I believe that we both work on it every day.

May 29, 2013
Wednesday

The month of May seems to have lasted about
five months, and the final end of the school
year cannot come soon enough for me. The
ending of my mother's life inside of mine has
taken nearly a year and continues even now. If I
am reconstituting our relationship, each of us
on a different side of the spiritual boundary,
then what exactly constitutes an ending of her
in my life? I could list a hundred ways, and I feel
her absence daily, but the ending of her, her
activity in my everyday life, seems more like a
small boat floating in the ocean — a small
definition of her presence, with a great deal of
life around it.

May 30, 2013
Thursday

This evening, driving home from a social function, I thought, "It's too late to call Mom, now," before realizing that I could not. The emotional perceptions always race ahead of the rational ones. Grief challenges one's emotional self to reconcile with one's rational, logical self – both have their own antennae but with different sensations of reality. After almost a year of my emotional and rational selves negotiating with one another, are they comfortable with their conclusions today?

Clearly, since the emotions' jurisdiction is not constrained by time, its view is more distant, perhaps sending itself across the border of the other side of life. Even so, there is always a day of absence to live through here, and each day continues some form of negotiation, even into the fullness of evening.

May 31, 2013
Friday

Every person who lives alone experiences loneliness at various times, I am certain. But once a journey through grief is begun, the slightest feeling of loneliness travels immediately downstream into an ocean of it. I begin to think that the continent on which I live is not the dominant topography; rather, it is a stopping point to pause, to rest, before launching off into the water again, at some mysterious juncture. Even on land, at night, I can always hear the waves.

I have happiness, to an extent, and laugh at something most days, but with no partner, no parents, and no children, those vast, moving, dark waters alone call me, the greatest depth in my immediate life.

June 1, 2013
Saturday

Today I attended a graduation Open House that I would have attended with my mother, and they would have been happiest to see my mother. It was a warm spring day, with children playing outside, young adults excited and happy at the life ahead of them, and a home abounding in gracious hospitality, yet only half of me walked into the house, the half clearer of grief, the half that some part of me has allocated for the daily intercourse of life. I interacted and conversed, meaningfully at times, and was glad I attended, leaving after an hour.

I wonder if others grieving feel as if they are in an invisible life, one that expands and includes two lives, so much of our interior life being distracting and rich, in its way. When, through some odd intersection with reality, our interior life connects to those outside of it, we can be confused, unsettled, unsure of how to situate ourselves. We are still living two lives – our own in the present and our life in the past, with our loved one; the emptiness demands this dual existence.

June 2, 2013
Sunday

My niece's twin boys were born this afternoon:
One was fine; the other is in an I.C.U.,
struggling to live.

I assume my mother and father know the
condition of the babies and the birth
complications. Can they offer special prayers
for them?

Those who are on the other side of life seem to
assume a new role to those they have left
behind – as if they become special intercessors
for prayer and assistance, or, at least, that's
how people sometimes think about them. And
are they available to help us? Guide us? Do
they then become more than human – or is
human more than we think it is?

I prefer to imagine my parents as they were in
life because that is what I can know best about
them, and there is plenty to think about with
the memories of a person's lifetime at one's
disposal.

Gradually, you begin to see through the
humidity of grief, as it dissipates, and can then
begin to intuit that wherever or whatever they
now are, there is something clear on the
horizon.

June 3, 2013
Monday

When something traumatic happens, it seems to cast you adrift from your own life. There is a sense of being dislocated, and your own life and habits become unfamiliar to you. I am now in the process of making my life become familiar to myself again, as if I have been traveling for a year and am now returning from a distant country. It is a curious sensation, in finding a motley pile of books you once read intently or seeing a project in the closet half-begun and abandoned. I see what needs to be done and even decide where or when to begin, but it feels as if I am moving in very slow motion – until I realize that I have only moved in my mind.

The finite world of death and growth is still galaxies away from the grief-recovering mind. I look pointedly at a star, as real and immediate as my teacup.

June 4, 2013
Tuesday

Today is my father's birthday, and this would have been a reason to celebrate at dinner, with raised wine glasses and a pecan pie laid by for dessert. Here we are, almost a decade later – my father departed this earth at 8:05 a.m. on Monday, September 15, 2003 – and instead I spend the day with people who never met him, and in the evening eat dinner alone.

It is no wonder that we cherish our stories; they define us to ourselves and remind us who to be. I was a daughter well-loved, strongly supported and cherished, one for whom my parents sacrificed much, as with my other siblings.

When I laid my ear against my father's chest at 8:06 that morning, the silence began then to instruct me: His love echoes through your own heart and expands into the universe. Inhabit it.

June 5, 2013
Wednesday

There was a strong confluence of memories this evening when my friend and I attended the Greek festival near my home. It was a year ago that we went without my mother for the first time, at the end of a long day at the hospital. My mother died four days later. In the years before that, Mom always went with us and loved the festival's food and music.

Grief turns us into observers; it stills our energy so that we watch the world moving by. We do not come home from work, walk in the door and set down our keys. We walk up to the door, only to realize there is no house. We have nothing to do but watch ourselves in our own life and wonder: Will the familiar associations of a loved one lost – a festival, a restaurant, a backyard deck – be emotionally jarring or a comfort? And how do we watch ourselves change?

June 6, 2013
Thursday

My friend, grieving deeply for her lost partner,
is not doing well, her son told me today. She
feels almost no will to live, he said, and I know
that feeling. A person in deep grief does not
feel apace with the rest of the world so
assumes she does not belong in it – what
difference if she is alive or not?

Where does our everyday life meet our soul?
How tender is that region between my present
self who is writing this and my spirit's territory?
That is the terrain we explore in grief, and it
demands a presence – and our full attention –
between our every common hour and our
seamless world of spirit.

June 7, 2013
Friday

I know my friend is entering the dense woods of the journey into grief, and I can only be here as a companion for her. I asked her this evening how her days were going, and she said that they were hard to get through.

As one who understands, I know that, for those in deep grief, the words of it they speak aloud feel like boulders that fall in front of them. Trying to articulate the experience – even to describe one day – is as if the words spoken slow down the words that dutifully follow after them; there is such depth of emotion behind each one that the pressure of that density compresses language, and words eventually slow to a halt.

Each day, she pushes into the underbrush of the forest and must find her way through; at some point, she will come to the clearing on the other side. She will emerge as a witness to the life inside its system, and her words will name every plant and creature she met within it. I am standing at the edge of my forest and know this.

June 8, 2013
Saturday

A year ago, every day was spent in the hospital, as we watched you decline, Mom. I know you remember those last two weeks of your life – difficult, uncomfortable, unpleasant, lonely, I am sure – and I hope you were comforted by our presence. It was just five days after this that you left us. I feel as if I have been holding onto a rope in the water every day since, hand-over-hand to get through each day. When it has been a year to the day, am I supposed to be able to let go?

Where are you?

What distance are you in? My own life is at a greater distance from myself, and I know you would understand.

June 9, 2013
Sunday

In our church, one of our parishioners, Jo, visits several gravestones every Sunday. Today I walked over to ask her about those gravestones. She explained each one – her grandparents, their daughter, her late husband. She sits on the bench and is quiet with them for a time.

Each of us in grief does that – in our minds, we sit at the stone and acknowledge the stillness there in our lives. Whether anyone can detect it or not, each of us sits there, in some region of our mind, every day, for a loved one who has died. Every day, a part of us is there, in a greening stillness.

June 10, 2013
Monday

It is raining steadily and has rained off and on much of the day. Such a cold, wet spring as we have had inspires a sort of pessimism that blurs other boundaries. I feel a kind of malaise, a grief weariness, and wonder: When the intensity of this condition begins to lessen, what will I be? Certainly not as I was before. I sometimes ask myself: If my mother could be here today, what would I do? Feel? Say? Would my grief lift away from me, for a moment?

It is a pleasant exercise, to imagine that, and I know my mother would enjoy my thinking this way. If that fleeting joy I feel with those questions is somehow transmitted to her, perhaps that is the transparent light of all true communication – both sides feel the warmth of love, across the dark sky of eternity.

June 11, 2013
Tuesday

Today outside the grocery store, I helped an elderly man by putting his shopping cart back with the others. At the moment I reached for the cart, I recognized him as one who lives at the senior community that my mother lived in. I had seen him there in the dining room and at other functions, many a day. I also knew that I could not open that topic in conversation with him, if he remembered me; I simply wasn't up to it.

I want to heal, to emerge into someone who can engage in such encounters with my former life with facility and grace. But if that state of being so healed ever comes, I suspect I will not be entirely there, as I once was, but someone similar to one they knew when I was sitting in that dining room, eating dinner with my mother, looking across the room. I am a being contained, out of context; I am no longer one brightened by a proximity to her. The newness of me is the same part of me that was always in relation to her, invisible in the glaring sunlight of the parking lot, as I walk to my car.

June 12, 2013
Wednesday

Tonight is one of the most still nights I have ever felt. Nothing seems to be stirring outside, not even a breeze to rustle the leaves. Am I stirring? Entangled amid these thoughts are those of my plans for the summer and of translating myself into a summer being. It is complicated, adjusting yourself, but each person must decide what condition she is in and what to do with oneself in each progressing season. Last summer, I was in the deep underwater regions of grief, but that condition gradually dissipated, and I now float on the surface on a raft. Maybe my mother will visit me there.

It was a year ago tonight when the nurse called me and said that my mother had passed away – it was 1:30 a.m., so actually June 13th. From that strange moment, my new life began, walking through a new air, as if a resounding meteor had suddenly tilted the earth off its axis and changed the atmospheric conditions.

No love, no devotion, no faith, no family can carry you back to your former life. No miracle can carry you back to your former self. Since then, every day, you seem to wake up in a different place, learning new customs, new faces, new habits, new ways of being. All the distance of the world is in your head, and if there is a destination, you have never known it.

June 13, 2013
Thursday

When I began this journal, more than five months ago, I planned to end it on this date, the anniversary of my mother's passing. My goal was to write in this journal every night, and I have achieved that, not missing a single daily entry since my first on January 6th.

It has helped my grief journey, which each of us takes alone, swimming into murky waters, unknown, unfamiliar, prompting confusion and anxiety. And since no one sees your condition, you feel especially alone, but this is not true. Loved ones, friends, colleagues – all have stories to tell, and I am humbled by them. I am sure my relationship with grief will change, but I will always be grateful for the hour or so I spent here every night with the freedom of my own thoughts.

I think of you today, Mom, and how deeply thankful I am that you loved books and reading and libraries and understood why we carried stacks of books to the circulation desk every week to check out. May God bless you this night and every evening into eternity; know that you are never more than a thought away, and that the brightness of you in my mind can lead me out of much darkness. We know what we had together, you and I, ever since I was a child, and my memory of that will warm many days.

May my words do you honor and continue to show me the way forward. I love you, and no time or presence will ever alter that. Love moves by its own day, in its own sky, I now know.

The Horizon

June 16, 2013
Sunday

It has been three days since I ended the regular entries in this journal, and tonight I realized that I was sad to see my regimen end, even though it has not been easy to maintain.

As long as I was writing, I was connected to my mother in the intimacy of that first year. I suppose that in the afterlife, our year on this side may not mean much, but what do I replace it with here? What fabric, from what day, do I create to replace the year that I just completed? What and where is the bond now? I feel that I would like to ask my mother for an active relationship, however she can manage it on her end, because I simply do not know if I have the wherewithal to bring something brand new forward. As at the beginning, I am displaced, disarmed, dazed. In fact, the "I" that I was has since dissolved, and she who writes this is undetermined, with parts undefined, watching the horizon from somewhere.

June 18, 2013
Tuesday

The Earth pulls me into its quiet, its day of a
thousand sparkling minutes in the sun and
shade, with birds, blossoms, leaves, worms – a
city of life out here – and all know their place in
that day's minutes. As I kneel into the soil,
briefly, repeatedly, I keep feeling the day as
settled time, as the peace that is under these
branches; if I am still and feel the melody of
light over my face, I am no longer alone.

Afterward
July 23, 2013

Today, in order to return the pacemaker checking device I found in my closet recently, I walked into the cardiology center where my mother got her blood levels checked every week for many years, since she was on Coumadin. I spoke to Naomi, the friendly nurse whom my mother was always happy to see; she was kind and gracious and spoke warmly of my mother. Then I felt inclined to visit Forwood Manor, where my mother lived for six years. I have driven by it weekly for thirteen months without being able to go in. But it was a perfect day: I spoke to Betty, at the front desk, and Kelly, from the office, and Ron, from the dining room, all in the lobby. They greeted me warmly, and I was very happy to see them. They spoke of my mother and her outgoing personality, her bright presence at Forwood, and everyone who loved her there; it was a great comfort. Before I left, I looked up at the window on the second floor landing, where she used to wave to me each time on my way out. I could easily imagine her there, waving and smiling.

I did not feel my mother's presence at Forwood Manor as much as I felt my own emerging. I walked into the present day, the past situated very securely within it, and my mind reconciled them both. I was floating on the water, resting in the tide, and I knew very completely: I have been loved enough to go forward, and I will honor that love. That's what the water was, all along. It enveloped me and carried me, and now I can breathe within it, and live, wherever I am.

One is ordained into grief, so to speak, and is thereby altered forever. But the deep love that inspired this "sea-change," as Shakespeare wrote, flows continuously through every continent of one's life, here and beyond. To those who grieve: You will never be the same, but the grief will reside in you, and the love will lap against it, for the rest of your days.

May the love, the truth, of your own days find you and keep you.

# # #

American Association of Pastoral Counselors:
http://www.aapc.org
The mission of the American Association of
Pastoral Counselors is to bring healing, hope,
and wholeness to individuals, families, and
communities by expanding and equipping
spiritually grounded and psychologically
informed care, counseling, and psychotherapy.

American Psychological Association:
http://www.apa.org
The American Psychological Association is the
largest scientific and professional organization
representing psychology in the United States.
Our mission is to advance the creation,
communication and application of
psychological knowledge to benefit society and
improve people's lives.

For more grief counseling resources, see also
the Office of Mental Health through your state
or local government, as well as places of
worship in your community.